Pasta

Pasta

Marlena Spieler

Photographs by Gus Filgate

headline

PHOTOGRAPHS © 2003 GUS FILGATE

FIRST PUBLISHED IN 2003
BY HEADLINE BOOK PUBLISHING

10 9 8 7 6 5 4 3 2 1

BRITISH LIBRARY CATALOGUING IN PUBLICATION DATA

Spieler, Marlena
Pasta
1. Cookery (Pasta)
I. Title
641.8'22

ISBN 0-7472-70279

PRINTED AND BOUND IN ITALY BY
G.CANALE & C.S.p.A
DESIGN BY DESIGN PRINCIPALS, WILTSHIRE

HEADLINE BOOK PUBLISHING
A DIVISION OF HODDER HEADLINE
338 EUSTON ROAD
LONDON NW1 3BH

www.headline.co.uk
www.hodderheadline.com

Contents

Acknowledgements 7

Introduction 9

A Bowl of Pasta Soup 24

Pasta from the Garden 45

Pasta from the Dairy 78

Pasta with Seafood 93

Pasta with Meats and Poultry 117

Quick, Quick Pasta 135

Big Baked Panfuls 154

Stuffed Pasta and Gnocchi 173

Index 190

ACKNOWLEDGEMENTS

To my pasta-eating daughter, Dr Leah Spieler, and her pasta-perfect partner, Jon Harford. To Alan McLaughlan, my husband, and to Gretchen Spieler, my stepdaughter.

Grazie mille to:
Publishing Director Heather Holden Brown, enthusiastic bundle of good energy, who said: 'Would you like to do a book on pasta?' (And, to further endear herself to me, she always laughs at my jokes.) Assistant Editor Juliana Lessa, who made the practical stuff happen with ease and delight; Assistant Production Director Nic Jones and Photographer Gus Filgate, Home Economist Linda Tubby, who made everything look as good as it tastes; my agents, Deborah McKenna Associates – Borra Garson, Martine Carter and Michelle, who keeps the admin in motion; the Italian Trade Commission including Antonietta Stefanic and her daughters, Charlotte and Caroline, and Patricia Carruthers.

Paolo Ardisson, friend and olive oil expert, of John Burgess Exports, as well as Isnardi/Ardoino Olive Oils, who press the sweet, fragrant oils from the Ligurian hills.

Jessica Mitchell, my Radio 4 producer on various *Food Programme* projects, for traipsing out to Genoa for the basil (oh, and that midnight swim in Portofino!); the wonderful Sheila Dillon of BBC Radio 4 *Food Programme*; and Greg and Charlie, presenters of *VegTalk* who ate my pasta and greens with great gusto 'live' on the radio. Thanks for letting me talk and cook, cook and talk, all of you!

Thanks to Antonio Carluccio for being a big dose of Italy in his every smile and hug; to Susanah Gelmetti and her wonderful crew for a week of eating and cooking in Italia; to Giorgio Locatelli, chef of London's Zafferano, for a marvellous pasta demonstration; and Valentina Harris for pesto in Portofino and being joyously Italian! Thanks also to Anna Kotwinzki at the Dialogue Agency for her delicious prosciutto and to Wild Card PR for supplying me with very fine Barilla pasta. Elaine Ashton provided a rainbow of pasta delights.

To friends: Kamala Friedman; Paula Aspin; Sandy Waks; MA Mariner and Rich Carreaga; Jerome Freeman and the late Sheila Hannon, much missed by us all; Dr Esther Novak and Reverend John Chendo; Paul Richardson; Dr Becky Brereton, whose middle name is Truffle; John and Mary Whiting; Nigel and Graham Gianni and Pamela Parmigiana; Ursula Ferrigno and Judy Ridgway; Amanda Hamilton and Tim Hemmeter; Phillip and Joyce Cecchettoroi.

Publications I have contributed throughout the year that I wrote this book including *The San Francisco Chronicle;* and my great editors and friends Michael Bauer, Miriam Morgan and Fran Irwin for sending me on a Roving Feast.

To my family, especially my parents, during this difficult year.

To the plucky and brave little pussycat, Madeline.

Introduction

A Pasta Feast

Picture this: a big bowl of pasta, set in the middle of the table, friends and family gathered around, forks in hand, inhaling the enticing fragrance while eagerly awaiting the first bite. Irresistible pasta, supple in texture and deliciously sauced, can put a smile on almost anyone's face – in Italy. Whether it be the olive oil-slicked Tuscan pasta, buttery Piedmontese, or the robust bowlfuls of Rome and Naples, each bite reeking deliciously of garlic, hot peppers, tomatoes, tasting of sunshine, grown men cheer at the mere thought – I see this all the time and I join in.

A feast of pasta has other appeals, too: it won't break the bank (unless you lavish expensive ingredients on it); it doesn't take much time (unless you decide to spend the afternoon rolling fettuccine or stuffing ravioli); and it is wonderful as a last-minute dish. It can also accommodate any level of cooking skills, from absolute beginner to inspired virtuoso, and all kinds of ingredients, from whatever you have left over in the fridge to exotic lobster, truffles or caviar. With pasta in your store cupboard you're never more than 10 minutes away from a dinner party.

Occasionally, when the urge for luxury and indulgence hits and wet, cold weather makes staying in the kitchen appealing, I roll up my sleeves and make a sumptuous pasta dish that takes time – lots of it. Time for cutting, chopping, rolling and stuffing. Enjoyable cooking time. This is pasta as a gastronomical thrill, rich and provocatively flavoured.

And you can make it all in advance – big panfuls layered with sauce, cheese, vegetables and/or meats. Lasagne, pasta *al forno*, crusty, cheesy macaroni gratins, cannelloni: simply having a pan in the oven is being halfway to a party.

Or start the party early and invite your friends to help mix up and roll out fresh home-made pasta, or simmer up a deliciously complicated sauce, or make a batch of home-made stuffed pastas such as ravioli or tortellini. Then sit down in front of the steaming dish of pasta, with a salad and a few bottles of wine, and tuck in. You don't need a formal place-setting, just a fork.

Pasta is truly a food for sharing, and if you eat it with gusto you will be a pleasure to share a meal with.

The Origins of Pasta

Contrary to popular myth, pasta was *not* brought from China to Italy by the Venetian traveller and writer Marco Polo (1254–1324); it is thought that he wrote about the noodles he ate there precisely because it was so much like the pasta of his homeland. In fact, pasta was possibly an invention of prehistoric people living in the Middle East and it is believed to be one of the first foods mankind created, tiny pellets of ground wheat mixed to a dough with water, cooked into little shapes, and an ancient ancestor of couscous.

There is evidence that by 100BC ancient Romans were eating thin strips of pasta called 'lagane', much like our modern lasagne and still eaten under its original name in parts of Italy. Etruscan tombs of the 4th century BC yielded pasta-making implements surprisingly like those we use today. The first mention of pasta in text, however, was written in Arabic, circa 1126, and found in Sicily.

Throughout what is now known as Italy, hand-rolled and chunky pasta (referred to as macaroni) was eaten with a variety of sauces and flavourings; for instance, in the area of Naples, the classic way to eat pasta during the Middle Ages was to dress it with its cooking water, grated cheese and black pepper. Garlic, onion, meat, fish and vegetables were also used when available.

In the 1600s the New World tomato was embraced by the population, especially around Naples, and by the 1700s tomato sauces were being used to create the classic Neapolitan pasta we know and love so well today. When pasta-loving King Ferdinand opened the first pasta factory, readily prepared pasta became easily available to everyone so the poor could now dig in to what had been food for the rich, and the wealthy were discovering the lusty joys of simple *pasta al pomodoro*, pasta with tomato sauce, until then only eaten by the poor.

As Italian emigrants settled far and wide in the latter centuries, they brought with them the flavours of their home. And in their new lands they cooked their traditional comforting dishes, adapting them to the foods available.

In some cases they started factories to produce their own pasta and, today, Australia exports not only durum wheat to Italy for making pasta, it sends its pasta there, too! In California there are few places you won't find fresh pasta, or restaurants specialising in it, and in Britain pasta has become an essential part of our diet. Additionally, with globalisation, pasta sauces have assimilated the exotic flavours of the world: chilli in Mexico and curry, cardamom and coriander in the East. Fusion flavours can be created by combining ingredients from different regions.

I feel privileged indeed to sit at Italy's table and share in her delicious food, absorbing her culture and vitality with each bite. I feel Italian in my soul when I am eating pasta; and sometimes I even look Italian, too!

In this book are some of my favourite recipes for pasta, garnered from my life at Italy's table and the Italian spirit that has seeped into my own cooking. I can think of nothing better than gathering my friends and family together in the kitchen, putting the water on to boil and awaiting the magic. As an Italian food magazine once said so perfectly: '*É sempre festa con la pasta*' – 'It is always a party when you are eating pasta'.

Pasta Fresca and Pasta Asciutta

Fresh pasta, *pasta fresca*, is home-made, fresh and tender. *Pasta asciutta* is dry, boiled only until it retains the little 'bite' at its heart; cooked this way it is called '*al dente*'.

Fresh pasta must be very good to be good. If you have access only to mediocre fresh pasta from the supermarket, give it a miss. Instead, choose a good-quality dried pasta. And many shapes of pasta are only at their satisfying best when they are dried: spaghetti, maccheroni, perciatelli, ziti, and so on; one of the reasons is that commercial dried pasta is made with semolina, which produces a firmer, toothsome dough. The water matters too (it is said that Abruzzo water is the best), as do the machine pieces from the pasta extruder. These extruding shapes must be made from expensive bronze, not a cheaper metal or plastic, for only the bronze gives the dough the rough, textured surface necessary to hold the sauce and moisture on to it; with a too-smooth pasta, the sauce will just slip off it, leaving a dull, flavourless dish.

Dried pasta comes in a huge variety of sizes and shapes, far too many to even list here. Then there are the many colours and flavourings, too, which keep increasing. In Puglia's Trulli, I saw little building-shaped pasta called trulli; in Siena there were naughty little penises. I've seen teddy bears and grape bunches, mushroom shapes, Christmas-tree shapes at Christmas, and the National Museum of Pasta in Rome has admitted to its selection of more than 700 shapes the e-pasta, an edible paean to the age of cyberspace, to signify computers. But these are silly amusements.

The truth is that the shape of a pasta really does make a difference to the way it pleases you. For instance, tubular shapes trap delicious bits and morsels in chunky sauces; long strands are good for absorbing juices of tomato sauces and seafood sauces without growing soft; while thicker pasta usually goes with strong, assertively flavoured sauces and delicate noodles with delicate sauces, such as cream, butter, and so forth (though tender eggy fettuccine is traditionally served with the robust meaty *ragù* of Bologna). These rules are passed down generation to generation; yet, like the Italians themselves, nothing remains stagnant, all is open to change and evolution.

But think about it: whereas spaghetti is terrific with anchovies, garlic and olive oil, a bowl of rigatoni or big chunks of pasta would be boring served so simply. And creamy sauces, so succulent on big shells, or on flat fettuccine, is just not right on spaghetti. Experience will tell all. Meanwhile, I've included lots of guidelines and suggestions.

Pasta Shapes and Sizes

Small shapes
Usually used for soups, but sometimes for other dishes too. Many shapes that are eaten in a large size with sauce are often eaten in smaller sizes in soups, such as penne (quills), sedani/sedanini (little celeries), cavatelli (small spirals), conchigliette (little shells), maccheroncini (elbows), farfalle (butterflies or bowties), orzo (rice-shaped pasta) and pasta such as stelline (little stars), alfabeti (little letters of the alphabet), ditalini/ditali (little fingers), semi di melone (shaped like melon seeds), chicchi di

pepe (little grains of pepper), anelli/anellini (little rings) – though these are also good cooked and layered with tomato and cheese for a Sicilian speciality – and others. Fregula is Sardinian, a couscous-like pasta eaten in soups and with seafood.

Long strands

Thin strands include capellini/capelli d'angelo (angel hair), spaghettini (thin strings), fedelini (little faithfuls), linguine (little flat tongues), bucatini (little holes), perciatelli (little 'pierced' strands), vermicelli (little worms), and so forth. Thicker strands include fettuccine (flat long ribbons), bavette (like fettuccine but wider), tagliatelle/tagliarini (like fettuccine but thinner), strangozzi/stringozzi/pici (fat types of spaghetti), pappardelle (fat ribbons), bigoli (fat long strands of buckwheat). The thinnest ones are used for clear and vegetable soups; the thicker ones in heartier vegetable and bean soups, often broken up into shorter lengths.

Thin strands, such as spaghettini, are best eaten with simple olive oil-based sauces with garlic, anchovy, tomato, seafood, pesto and so forth. Thicker spaghetti holds up well with meaty sauces.

Tubular shapes

Most tubular pasta is good with hearty sauces containing minced meat, bits of sausage, chunks of vegetables or perhaps baked in a casserole. Tubetti (the largest), maccheroni/maccheroncini (elbows), ziti, tortiglioni or rigatoni (fat ridged tubes), penne (quills), and penne rigate (*rigate*, by the way, means 'ridged') are perfect examples. Bucatini are long tubular strands. Candele are enormously round and very long. Eaten in Puglia, they are simply huge bucatini. Perciatelli, also known as bucatini for the hole in the middle (*buco* means hole), are big, fat, spaghetti-like strings of varying thicknesses.

Other chunky shapes

These include lumachelle/lumachine (curled, hollow snail shapes), Gigli (lillies), orecchiette (flat, slightly curled discs, like little ears), trofie (unevenly shaped corkscrew pasta), cavatelli (little hollowed-out ovals) and gnocchetti (curled shells). When fresh, cavatelli are known as strozzapreti, literally meaning 'priest-stranglers' (though no one is sure exactly why). Others are gemelli or twins (chunky pasta twists wrapped twinlike around each other), and caserecci, fusilli and fusilli lunghi, which are different types of twists. There are farfalle (butterflies or bowties, which come in a wide variety of sizes), conchiglie (shells) and cavatappi (corkscrews). Cars are well represented in Italian pasta cuisine: rotelle (little wheels) and radiatore (little radiators) are both delicious with robust sauces. Some shapes are good with cream, vegetables and cheese, while others are good with vegetables and tomatoes; they all need a sauce with big flavour to keep the pasta from overpowering them. In Puglia you'll also find orecchiette grandi, or 'big ears' – huge, round, cuplike pastas, which are first boiled then stuffed and baked.

The Secrets of Perfect Pasta

1. The usual recommendation is to allow about 100g (4 oz) of pasta per person – more or less according to appetite.

2. Allow lots of water – say, 1.5 litres (2¾ pints) for each 300–400g (11–14 oz) of dried pasta, or 500g (1 lb 2 oz) of fresh pasta; use more if you have a pan big enough. You need lots of water for it to travel all over the pasta, cooking it evenly and leaving it fresh, not gummy. A tablespoon of salt must be added to each litre (1¾ pints) of water; without it, the pasta will taste bland.

3. Be sure the water is at a rolling boil before adding all the pasta at once. If it is not boiling, the pasta will become gummy as the outer layer of starch turns soggy. When the pasta is added to the water it will stop boiling; let it return to the boil then lower the heat slightly to keep it at a slower but continuous rolling boil until it is cooked, taking care that it doesn't bubble over.

4. Do not overcook! In fact, undercook pasta slightly as it will continue to cook in the hot sauce while waiting to be served. You can tell when it's ready by taste. It should literally be *al dente*, 'to the tooth', with a bit of bite left in it. Fresh pasta should be delicate and tender, not mushy.

5. Remove the pasta from the heat a minute or two before it is *al dente*; the heat of the water will continue to cook it. One method I learned in Rome was to boil the pasta furiously for several minutes then leave it to sit for up to 5 or 6 minutes.

6. Save a few tablespoons of the pasta's cooking water to add to the sauce when you toss it together. It makes a liaison between sauce and pasta, turning them into one harmonious bowlful rather than a plate of pasta topped with sauce. It is very important to add this hot cooking water: the pasta will absorb about 20 per cent of the sauce it is served with in the few minutes after it has been tipped on to the serving dish. This can result in a gummy, dryish dish.

How to Make Pasta

Forget an expensive extruding electrical whizzbang of a pasta machine; instead, buy a good hand-cranked one that rolls the dough into thin noodles. It will not break the bank and will never fall apart or need parts replacing.

Home-made, fresh-rolled pasta is normally far better than fresh bought pasta and, once learned and demystified, pasta-making is a great cooking skill to have. You can roll the dough into lasagne, cannelloni, yummy ravioli, or fettuccine as delicate as only home-rolled can be. Alternatively, you can form shapes with your hands such as orecchiette and fusilli (*see page 12*).

When making pasta, it's best to leave the dough to sit for an hour or so before rolling it out, to give the gluten a chance to relax and lighten up so that the dough is more tender and easier to work with. Sometimes I make the dough a day in advance and store it in the refrigerator, but before rolling it out it's important to flour the work surface and rolling pin generously, to allow for the dampness that results from the dough being chilled.

As for the leftover bits of pasta after you've cut your shapes, lay them out on a wire rack and dry them, then store them in your *pasta mista* jars.

Pasta Fresca
Fresh Eggless Pasta

Fresh pasta made with only flour, water and a dribble of olive oil is popular in Italy. This eggless pasta is white, slightly doughy and perfect for many of the thick, chewy traditional pasta dishes of the Italian country kitchen.

I also find that an eggless pasta is good for non-Italian dishes. It works really well when rolled into the Japanese udon-type noodles, or cut into fettuccine – or tagliatelle – like strips, and boiled, then dressed with soy sauce, sesame oil and sliced spring onions.
SERVES 4–6

500g (1 lb 2 oz) plain Italian flour
Pinch of salt
150–200ml (5–7 fl oz) water, or as needed
50ml (2 fl oz) extra virgin olive oil

Place the flour and salt in a large bowl and make a well in the centre. Gradually add the water and olive oil, stirring continuously, until it forms a stickyish though stiff dough. Knead it heartily until it is very smooth, adding more flour if it is too wet or a little more water if too dry.

Alternatively, to make the dough in a food processor, place the flour in the bowl and, with the machine on, gradually add the liquid. Remove the dough and knead as above.

Place the dough in a plastic bag or covered glass bowl and leave to sit for up to 2 hours, or in the refrigerator for up to 2 days.

When ready to use, remove an egg-sized piece of dough, keeping the rest covered to stay moist. Either roll it out through a pasta machine (*see page 16*) or form shapes by hand. Shapes most suitable for eggless pasta dough are fusilli *fatti a mano* (hand made), orzo (rice-shaped pasta), strangozzi and orecchiette (*see pages 11–12*).

Pasta all'Uovo Fresca
Fresh Egg Pasta

Tender eggy noodles, supple and golden, are the glory of the table when cloaked in either butter and cheese or in a classic tomatoey, meaty ragù, Bolognese-style. In Florence I love eating at the Castello Sorci, where the golden eggy tagliatelle is delicious and enticing.

In general, egg pasta takes about 100g (4 oz) of flour per egg. It is more elastic than the eggless variety and is best made into long ribbons rather than chunky shapes.

SERVES 4

450g (1 lb) plain Italian flour
4 eggs
Pinch of salt
1 tablespoon water

Heap the flour into a pile on a work surface, then make a well in the centre and break the eggs into it. Add the salt and water, and with a fork start lightly beating the eggs with the water, gradually incorporating the flour from the edges until it is too stiff to fork, then mix with your hands. Or you can mix the eggs with your fingers, incorporating the flour as you do so. Alternatively, blend the ingredients in a food processor or mixer until it has formed a stiff dough.

Knead the dough until it is smooth and shiny, either by hand or in a pasta machine. If possible, wrap the dough in clingfilm and rest it in the fridge for half an hour as this makes it more pliable.

COLOURFUL VARIATIONS

Pasta Nera: for a blackish/greyish eggless pasta, add ink of squid, substituting about 2 tablespoons of liquid for each egg, adding more if you need to.

Pasta all'Erbe: for a delightful green-flecked pasta, knead in several handfuls of finely chopped or puréed basil, thyme, parsley or rocket to the dough. If it seems too wet, add a little more flour when kneading.

Pasta al Basilico: purée 3-4 tablespoons of fresh basil with 1 tablespoon of olive oil and add to the flour mixture.

Pasta allo Zafferano: boil 5 tablespoons of water with several large pinches of saffron for a few minutes then leave to sit and colour the water yellow; this should take about 30 minutes. Add it to the dough along with the eggs and proceed as above, adding a little extra flour if needed.

Pasta Verde: add 4–6 tablespoons of puréed, well-drained spinach to the flour in place of one of the eggs.

Pasta Rossa: add 2–3 tablespoons of tomato purée in place of one of the eggs.

Using a Pasta Machine

To knead the dough, cut off a lemon-sized piece of dough and flatten it slightly. Rub it with a bit of flour. Set the machine's rollers on the largest opening and feed the dough through over and over again, about ten times, until it has become a shiny and elastic rectangular shape.

To roll out the dough, adjust the machine to the next-thickest setting and roll the dough through, then set it one level thinner and roll it through again. Adjust the machine to a thinner setting each time and the dough will lengthen and flatten as you roll it through the various sizes.

For fettuccine and most other pastas, stop when you've rolled it through the second-thinnest setting. The last setting is for a very delicate pasta and is too fine for most. For a hearty pasta such as ravioli, the third-thinnest setting is usually best.

If you are using your sheets of pasta (*sfoglie*) to make ravioli or other shapes, use each one as soon as it comes out to prevent it drying.

If you are cutting the dough into strips, leave them to dry for a short while, around 5–10 minutes, before cooking. This stabilises the dough and helps it hold together.

Three Simple Tomato Sauces

A good tomato sauce complements pasta perfectly, and below are three that not only demand little from the cook but are also excellent tossed with either thin strands of spaghetti or fat penne, poured over plump stuffed ravioloni, around Sicilian-style aubergines or crowned with shreds of salty cheese, *alla Napoletana*.

Two of the recipes use canned tomatoes and the last uses fresh. Canned tomatoes are an Italian staple and the Neapolitans raise them to great gastronomic heights, as anyone who's tasted a home-preserved Neapolitan tomato will testify.

It only takes the addition of a very few ingredients to transform a tomato sauce and make it different from the next one: a little onion, a little garlic, a handful of herbs. Simmer fresh tomatoes into a lovely light sauce, taste it, then add a handful of sweet basil – you will be amazed at the difference.

Time, too, is a great transformer: simmer tomatoes for only a few minutes and you have a light, simple sauce. Cook it for longer and the sauce becomes richer and thicker, until you have an intensely flavoured virtual tomato purée. Continue the cooking for longer still and you will end up with a dark, thick paste, the *estratto* of Italy's south, to add to dishes in tiny spoonfuls here and there.

Salsa al Pomodoro
Tomato Sauce

SERVES 4

1 can tomatoes (about 400g/14 oz)
½ onion, chopped
2 cloves garlic, halved
½ stalk celery, chopped (optional)
Pinch of salt
Freshly ground black pepper
¼–½ teaspoon sugar, or to taste
2 tablespoons extra virgin olive oil

In a food processor or blender, whizz the tomatoes with their juice to a purée. Tip it into a saucepan with the rest of the ingredients and cook for about 15–20 minutes over a medium heat, stirring, until the vegetables are soft and the sauce flavourful.

Strain or blend again if desired for a smooth texture, or leave chunky.

Salsa al Pomodoro e Basilico
Tomato Sauce with Basil

SERVES 4

1 can tomatoes (about 400g/14 oz)
1 clove garlic, thinly sliced
Pinch of salt
Freshly ground black pepper
¼–½ teaspoon sugar, or to taste
Several leaves fresh basil
2 tablespoons extra virgin olive oil

In a food processor or blender, whizz the tomatoes with their juice to a purée. Tip it into a saucepan with the rest of the ingredients, bring to the boil then reduce the heat and simmer for about 15–20 minutes until the sauce is reduced in volume and concentrated in flavour.

Salsa di Pomodori Freschi
Fresh Tomato Sauce from Napoli

SERVES 4

450g (1 lb) ripe, flavourful tomatoes, quartered
Pinch of salt
Freshly ground black pepper
¼–½ teaspoon sugar, or to taste
1–2 tablespoons extra virgin olive oil
Few leaves fresh basil

Purée the tomatoes in a food processor, then pour into saucepan. Season with salt, pepper and a little sugar and place over a medium-low heat. When the tomatoes are simmering, lower the heat right down to avoid burning the sauce and continue to simmer for about 20 minutes or until it has thickened.

Remove from the heat, stir in the olive oil and basil, and serve.

Pesto Sauces

From the word *pestare*, which means to crush or pound, comes the classic sauce of crushed or pounded basil we know and love as pesto. It is said that pesto originated as a sauce in ancient Rome and was adapted by the people of the many regions of what is now known as Italy. Others say that pesto came from Liguria and that its sea-faring people spread the idea to other far-flung places. (Apparently Christopher Columbus carried pesto with him when he set sail on his last voyage to the New World.)

Although you can buy some quite good brands of bottled pesto, when it is basil season, make your own: it is sublime. (Or at least as good as the basil you find.)

In Liguria they say that to make proper pesto you must pick only the basil that grows on the west side of the Ligurian hills, because this has the best sun and the best fragrance! Ligurian basil is sweet, fragrant and distinctive, whereas other types of basil can have too much of an aniseed or minty flavour. Add just a few sprigs of parsley, a grating of Parmesan or pecorino romano (*see page 20*), and pour in some sweet Ligurian olive oil – amazingly, pesto made with olive oil from other regions, no matter how good it is, just doesn't taste right.

Pesto is best eaten with thin, long strands of pasta. If you would rather not include pine nuts in the pesto, you can scatter them separately over the pasta before serving.

Pesto

SERVES 4

2–5 cloves garlic
125ml (4½ fl oz) extra virgin olive oil, preferably Ligurian, plus extra to
    cover
2–3 tablespoons raw pine nuts
3–4 large bunches of fresh basil, leaves removed from the stems
Salt
85–100g (3½–4 oz) Parmesan cheese, freshly grated

Make the pesto in a food processor. Place the garlic in the bowl and whizz until finely chopped, then add the olive oil, pine nuts and basil and blend to a purée. Add salt and Parmesan to taste, pour into jars or bowls and cover with a slick of extra olive oil.

Pesto freezes extremely well, even better without garlic and cheese, which should then be added after defrosting.

VARIATION

Tuscan Pesto

Tuscany borders on Liguria and in this area you'll find pesto made with walnuts. For such a pesto, simply substitute the pine nuts with chopped walnuts.

A NOTE ABOUT INGREDIENTS USED IN THE RECIPES

All salt is sea salt, preferably coarse grains or flakes.

All pepper is freshly ground black pepper – when it is freshly ground you get the lovely pepper fragrance and flavour instead of just heat.

All olive oil is extra virgin unless otherwise specified. Always buy the most intensely flavoured olive oil you can find. Sometimes it will be the most expensive, but not always.

If you can't get hold of the type of pasta specified in any of the recipes, substitute with another in the same category as outlined on pages 11-12. It will work just as well.

La Dispensa: the Pasta Pantry

Anchovies (*alici*, *acciughe* and numerous other spellings): tiny little fish preserved in salt or oil, add great briny flavour to pasta. Sometimes you can find fresh anchovies, silky and shimmery, great to be simply filleted, lightly marinated, then popped into the mouth, or heaped on to bruschetta or a bowl of pasta.

Basil: fresh basil, sweet leaves of basil, a must for the Italian summer table. Crush them in your hands and scatter them over any pasta and tomato dish. Chop them finely and douse them with olive oil then toss with pasta. Stir them into tomatoes and seafood as it simmers. Enjoy fresh basil whenever you can - dried basil is not an option.

There are many types of basil. Some, from the south, have a minty flavour, or a peppery one, or taste of aniseed; the best basil is from Liguria, with a distinctively sweet flavour.

Beans: beans, beans, beans! A shelf filled with an assortment of pulses, both dried and canned, means a potential sauce for pasta is always available – a rustic, hearty, healthy meal. And, if you use canned beans, quick pasta. Chickpeas, borlotti beans and cannellini beans are all indispensable to your pasta kitchen.

Breadcrumbs: grate dried good bread – the best bread you can find – on the large holes of a grater. Good bread makes great breadcrumbs and it is amazing the variety of dishes you can use them in. When toasted or fried in olive oil until crispy brown, they are called *pangrattato*, great for sprinkling on top of pasta.

Capers: salted ones are preferable to those preserved in brine. Soak them in cold water for about 10 minutes then drain well and use. If they are very salty, soak for longer in fresh water.

Cheeses (*formaggi*): good-quality Parmesan is a dream – grate it, shred it, shave it, chop it finely; it combines with almost every delicious thing you can toss pasta with (except fish and shellfish dishes, which usually eschew the cheese). Parmesan, the real Parmesan (Parmigiano Reggiano), is as expensive as it is delicious. Some countries have domestic Parmesans that vary in quality. There are other cheeses that are also wonderful for grating on to pasta: grana padano is a Parmesan-type cheese of almost similar quality; asiago is blander but delicious; and in America, dry jack is quite good.

Pecorino is marvellous, made from ewe's milk (*pecora*) and varies in texture as it ages; from quite fresh when new to hard and pungent when mature. If you can find truffled pecorino, buy it! Grate it on to hot chunky pasta, such as caserecci, doused with olive oil, then toss the whole thing with chopped rocket. Pecorino romano is a hard sheep's cheese with a delicious full flavour; excellent in place of Parmesan or grana padano, and slightly less expensive.

Mozzarella, fresh and milky balls of tender, chewy cheese that melts into a stringy delight; at its best when made with buffalo milk. In its home territory on the Amalfi coast, buffalo mozzarella is judged by its age: like fresh bread, when more than a few hours old it is past its best.

Provolone is a semi-firm, pleasantly mild cheese, excellent for slicing or shredding and melting on top of a pasta casserole, or into a *timballo* (a mould of pasta) or even in a *panino* (sandwich).

Caciocavallo is a hard cheese (similar to provolone) which is rich in flavour yet light rather than heavy and fatty; it is delicious sliced and layered in baked pasta, or shredded into pasta with fried courgettes or aubergine. In Sicily, primosale is a similar type of cheese, but very mild and light and quite fresh; sample it drizzled with freshly pressed olive oil and a handful of olives alongside.

Gorgonzola is the famous blue cheese of Italy's Lombardy. Mascarpone is an unfermented thick double cream cheese, delicious spooned and melted over a bowl of hot pasta. Goat and cow ricotta, cottage-type cheeses, fresh and aged, are made in Sicily; salted ricotta is marvellous to grate over a bowl of pasta and aubergines.

Quatirolo is similar to feta and has a refreshing character. Fontina is another northern cheese, rich and nutty and so luscious to melt with hot, rich and creamy pasta. And taleggio is a soft, gooey cheese, rich and unctuous and delightfully meltable.

The region of Piedmont produces myriad cheeses, and in the way of its French neighbours across the border, follows the tradition of offering the cheeseboard during a meal. Most of these cheeses do not travel outside their region, and many are unique to their locality. Some are so amazingly strong that you won't even need to have the cheese trolley brought to you – it can come on its own!

Smoked cheeses such as provolone, mozzarella and the like are often used in Campania and other regions of the south. They have a distinctive smoky flavour and firm texture. I prefer them on their own rather than in pasta dishes, but they are often diced and folded into a mixture for a baked pasta or a simple tomato sauce.

Chillies, fresh or dried: peperoncino or hot-pepper flakes are what the Italians use for chillies in quite a few dishes, depending on the area. In the south, say in Puglia and Calabria, expect to find a fiery flavour here and there, especially in salami. In other areas, the peperoncino only adds a piquant accent, unless you are speaking of a special dish such as pasta arrabbiata. If you are visiting Italy it's definitely worth bringing back a peperoncino or two.

Take care when cooking with chillies that the vapours don't irritate your eyes (I often use safety goggles when I'm frying hot peppers or chillies) and lungs. Wash your hands well after preparing them.

Garlic: buy it fresh, use it often (though I use it probably more often then even the most ardent Sicilian). Fresh garlic should be firm to the squeeze; soft cloves indicate rot and must be thrown away. When you open them up they should have a good whiteish colour; if they are brown, they are too old. Never chop a large amount of garlic and keep it in olive oil; you might be able to buy such a product commercially but the garlic will have been heat-treated to stop spoilage. Fresh garlic packed into olive oil at home is a dangerous medium for botulism; always throw away any garlic that has sat in olive oil for longer than two weeks. In my home one week is the most I'll keep any garlic preparation.

Herbs: in addition to fresh basil, fresh parsley is indispensable in the Italian kitchen. Flat-leaf parsley has the most flavour and texture. Fresh marjoram, oregano (it *must* be Italian), rosemary, sage and thyme all add flavour to the pasta pot. You can also buy them dried in an Italian dried-herb combination.

Olive oil: use only the best, most flavourful, freshest olive oil for your pasta. Anything less will be second rate. Top-quality pasta tossed with excellent olive oil is a meal in itself.

Most – but not all – of the best olive oils will be extra virgin. Many virgin olive oils are excellent and are still cold pressed but have a slightly higher acidity rating than extra virgin. There are even one or two ordinary olive oils that are terrific – and many extra virgins that disappoint. Whatever the quality or source, you must know how to store the oil – in a dark, cool place, as light destroys the oil's good flavour and freshness.

Olives: to choose olives is really a matter of taste. Italy produces many varieties, as do France, Spain, Greece, the Middle East, North Africa and California.

Black or green, their flavour and appeal will depend upon their type, the way they are cured, where they are grown, their size and so forth. The recipes in this book usually stipulate very loosely which type to go for; otherwise, you are on your own, armed with your tastebuds. If it's delicious in your mouth, it will be delicious in your pasta.

Olive paste: or, if anchovies are added, tapenade. This is a paste of olives, either green or black, sometimes with olive oil or garlic, herbs, chilli, etc., added. Olive paste adds a big hit of flavour to a dish – stir in a spoonful with pasta and goat's cheese, pasta and tomato sauce, pasta and lemon or tuna or herbs.

Pancetta: Italian bacon which is marinated with herbs and other flavourings.

Pesto: a jar or two of good pesto is invaluable in your store cupboard. Even if you prefer to make your own, it is marvellous to have some to stir into a tomato sauce, a bowl of pasta and vegetables, or a bowl of minestrone at a moment's notice.

Prosciutto: Italian ham. The best are raw and air-dried and include Parma and San Daniele.

Stock: good home-made stock is delicious with pasta – boil it down and turn it into a sauce, or simmer it and float a handful of pasta in it. Many shops sell fresh stock these days and I am quite fond of a liquid concentrated stock that comes in vegetable, beef, chicken and fish flavours and isn't as salty as the cubes. Porcini stock cubes from Italy, available at some delis, are so full of wild mushroom flavour, albeit rather salty, that I recommend them. Just adjust the salt in the dish accordingly.

Saffron: noticeable for its bright-yellow colour, it imparts a unique, slightly sweet, slightly medicinal aroma and flavour. It is delicious with seafood, cream, tomatoes, rocket, chicken and pasta. Though the best saffron from other countries is usually sold in threads, Italian saffron is often sold in powder form. San Gimignano in Tuscany is known for its saffron-tinted pasta specialities.

Sardines: always keep a can or two of sardines in your store cupboard. Like tuna, you never know when they'll make the best midnight pasta you could want.

Sun-dried tomatoes: chewy desiccated tomatoes, though some are chewier than others. Buy them dried or in jars, rehydrated, marinated, and similar in character to olives. Sun-dried tomatoes in their dry state make a great addition to sauces and some pastas; in their marinated state they add oomph to dishes like roasted peppers, pasta with sauces and tuna.

Sun-dried vegetables: aubergines and peppers are also sun-dried along with tomatoes. They have a leathery, chewy, brittle consistency and last for ever, needing to be rehydrated in water before being cooked up with the other ingredients.

Tomatoes: fresh tomatoes are wonderful in season. Cherry tomatoes tend to be reliably good whereas other varieties tend to be more variable in flavour. Canned tomatoes are also wonderful and a principal ingredient in the Italian store cupboard. When I am starving and can think of nothing to make for supper, I know that a can of tomatoes and a packet of pasta will feed me well. Always keep several cans on your shelf, whole or chopped, although I usually avoid additions such as herbs, garlic, etc.

Passata (puréed tomatoes), both in the carton and jar, is excellent too and should be part of your pasta pantry, as should tomato purée.

Tuna: add canned tuna to a tomato sauce, or just tip it into plain spaghetti with garlic, parsley and olive oil. The important thing is to choose good tuna – I like the kind canned in olive oil best.

A Bowl of Pasta Soup

On a cold night, a bowl of hot soup with pasta is one of life's most comforting foods; equally, on a hot and sultry day a bowl of cool minestrone, scented with pesto, can be utterly reviving.

Italians traditionally begin a meal with soup. It is considered an alternative to pasta, although more often than not it will have pasta in it, as the soups in this chapter do. In fact, pasta with a sauce is generally called *pasta asciutta*, to distinguish it from pasta in soup.

A big bubbling pan of soup studded with chewy bites of pasta can be a meal in itself, and the variety is endless. In fact, you need nothing more showy than a pot of very clear, very delicious stock. Don't go overboard. Let the excellent quality of simplicity show through.

Three Simple Soups that You Might Not Have Thought of

Minestra di Pasta e Broccoli
Spaghetti and Broccoli Soup

SERVES 4

Simmer a head of diced broccoli, including the peeled stems, along with a handful of broken spaghetti in 1.5 litres (2¾ pints) fish or chicken stock, until both are tender. Add a little thinly sliced garlic as it cooks, if you like.

Serve in bowls, drizzled with extra virgin olive oil, and, if you are using chicken stock rather than fish, add freshly grated Parmesan cheese to taste.

Minestra di Ceci e Orzo
Chickpea Soup with Orzo

SERVES 4

Boil 1 litre (1¾ pints) chicken or vegetable stock with 400g of canned chickpeas, drained, and 250g (9 oz) orzo, a clove or two of thinly sliced garlic and a few sprigs of fresh fennel leaves, chopped. Cook until the orzo is *al dente*, then remove from heat and serve with extra fresh fennel leaves sprinkled over and freshly grated Parmesan cheese if desired.

Raviolini con Formaggio di Capra in Brodo di Pollo
Goat's Cheese Raviolini in Chicken Soup

SERVES 4

Bring 1 litre (1¾ pints) of chicken stock to the boil. Meanwhile, cook goats' cheese raviolini (which you can buy dried in packets) in rapidly boiling salted water until they are just *al dente*. Drain carefully and lower them into the simmering stock. Serve the soup sprinkled generously with chives and freshly chopped tarragon.

Acquacotta con Pasta e Rucola

Tuscan Tomato and Potato Soup with Pasta and Rocket

This cheerful little soup is easy to prepare and, as well as being delicious served up hot and steamy, it is also good eaten cool on a blisteringly hot summer's day.

Acquacotta means simply 'cooked water' but, although this is indeed a simple soup, it is one rich with country flavours and spicy enough to make you reach for the wine.
SERVES 4

1 large potato (about 300g/11 oz), peeled and cut into thick slices
1.5 litres (2¾ pints) vegetable stock, plus extra water if needed
2 ripe tomatoes, chopped
150g (5 oz) conchigliette (small shells)
3 tablespoons extra virgin olive oil
3 cloves garlic, finely chopped
Pinch or two of crumbled dried chilli
50g (2 oz) wild rocket leaves, cut up coarsely
Parmesan or pecorino cheese, to serve

Place the potato, stock and tomatoes in a large saucepan and bring to the boil. Cook until the potato is tender, about 15 minutes. Still on the heat, mash a few of the potato slices, then add the pasta to the simmering liquid.

Meanwhile, in a small saucepan or frying pan, gently heat together the oil, garlic and chilli until fragrant but not browned. Remove from the heat.

When the pasta is just *al dente*, add the rocket leaves to the hot soup, along with the fragrant oil. Stir a few minutes to wilt the rocket, then ladle into bowls, and serve each one with Parmesan cheese. Though you might prefer freshly grated Parmesan, I like to crumble some of it into the soup and grate the rest so that the occasional bit of cheese bursts into flavour in my mouth.

Acquacotta alla Scansano

Tuscan Spinach Soup with Porcini, White Beans and Shells

This lusty Tuscan country soup is often served with big hunks of unsalted Tuscan bread soaked in it. I once ate a super version in the Maremma, at Antico Casale di Scansano, and followed it up with a long soak in the hot springs of Saturnia.
SERVES 4

1 onion, finely chopped
5 cloves garlic, finely chopped
3–4 tablespoons extra virgin olive oil
100g (4 oz) fresh spinach leaves, coarsely chopped
200g (7 oz) fresh or canned tomatoes, chopped
20g (¾ oz) dried porcini mushrooms, broken into tiny pieces
1 litre (1¾ pints) vegetable or chicken stock
Salt and freshly ground black pepper
1–2 tablespoons freshly chopped parsley
100g (4 oz) conchigliette (small shells)
400g (14 oz) canned cannellini beans, drained
Freshly grated Parmesan cheese for sprinkling

Lightly sauté the onion and garlic in the olive oil in a large pan until softened, then add the spinach, tomatoes, porcini and stock. Bring to the boil, then reduce the heat and simmer for about 10 minutes or until the mushroom pieces are tender and the soup tastes flavourful. Season to taste, and add the parsley.

Meanwhile, in another large pan, cook the pasta in rapidly boiling salted water until nearly *al dente*. Drain, add to the soup with the beans, and simmer for a further 5–10 minutes or until the pasta is completely cooked.

Serve hot in bowls with Parmesan grated on top.

Minestra di Fave e Ditalini

Broad Bean and Potato Soup with Tomatoes and Ditalini

Pale-green broad beans with dots of red tomato make for a very appealing and simple soup. Ah, but not a speedy one: you do need to peel fresh broad beans first, to release the delicate tiny bean inside the tough indigestible skin and give the soup real finesse.

You can use fresh beans, as described here, frozen, or even canned . With the latter, there's no need to parboil; simply drain them and shell them.

SERVES 4

300g (11 oz) podded broad beans
Salt
4–5 spring onions, thinly sliced
4–5 cloves garlic, coarsely chopped
4 tablespoons extra virgin olive oil, plus extra for drizzling
125ml (4½ fl oz) dry white wine
1 litre (1¾ pints) vegetable stock
1 medium-to-large potato, peeled and diced
3 ripe tomatoes, chopped
200g (7 oz) ditalini (little fingers)
Freshly grated Parmesan cheese, as desired

To skin the broad beans, blanch them for 5–7 minutes in a pan of lightly salted boiling water until they are just tender. Take them off the heat, drain and rinse in cold water and when cool remove the skins.

Meanwhile, in a large pan, lightly sauté the spring onions and garlic in half the olive oil until the onions are softened, then pour in the wine. Cook over a high heat until the wine has reduced by about half; this should take only a few minutes.

Add the stock and potato and simmer for about 30 minutes or until the potato is mushy. Add the broad beans, tomatoes and remaining olive oil and cook over a high heat for 5 minutes or just long enough to bring the flavours together and slightly cook the tomatoes (you want them to keep some of their fresh character). Remove from the heat and set aside.

In another large pan, cook the pasta in rapidly boiling salted water until almost *al dente*. Drain, then add to the soup, return it to the heat and warm through for about 5 minutes until the pasta is *al dente* and the soup is rich and flavourful. If it is too thick and concentrated, thin it down with some hot water that the pasta was cooked in.

Serve right away, with Parmesan and extra olive oil sprinkled into each bowl.

Minestra di Asparagi con Stelline

Asparagus Soup with Star-shaped Pasta

Light consommé, studded with bites of asparagus and a constellation of tiny pasta stars or stelline. If you can't find stelline, however, use any tiny soup pasta you like. A squirt of lime and a sprinkling of grated cheese enliven this simple and wholesome soup.

SERVES 4

2 shallots, finely chopped
1–2 tablespoons extra virgin olive oil
3 cloves garlic, finely chopped
1½–2 bundles of asparagus, tough stalks removed, the rest cut into bite-sized pieces
1.5 litres (2¾ pints) chicken or vegetable stock
150–200g (5–7 oz) stelline (little stars)
Salt and freshly ground black pepper
1–2 limes, cut into wedges
Freshly grated Parmesan cheese, as desired

Lightly sauté the shallots in the olive oil in a large pan until softened, then add the garlic and half the asparagus and cook for a few moments to bring out the flavour of the garlic but not to brown it.

Add the stock and stelline and bring to the boil. Cook on a high heat for about 3 minutes then add the rest of the asparagus and simmer for a few more minutes or until all the asparagus is just cooked.

Taste for seasoning and ladle into bowls, serving each with a wedge of lime squeezed into the soup and a sprinkling of Parmesan.

Minestra Giardiniera

Yellow and Green Bean Soup with Ditalini

Tender strands of fresh beans – use both yellow and green if you can find them, or just the green ones if not – enhance this simple soup, with a final flourish of warmed garlic-flavoured olive oil.

SERVES 4

1 litre (1¾ pints) chicken or vegetable stock
6 cloves garlic, thinly sliced
1 small carrot, finely chopped
1 stalk celery, thinly sliced
4–5 ripe medium-sized tomatoes, chopped
125–150g (4½–5 oz) ditalini (little fingers) or similar
125g (4½ oz) each of tender yellow and green beans (wax or fine/dwarf
    beans), trimmed and cut into bite-sized pieces
1 teaspoon freshly chopped rosemary
3–4 tablespoons extra virgin olive oil
Salt and freshly ground black pepper

Place the stock in a large pan with half the garlic and all the carrot, celery and tomatoes and bring to the boil. Cook over a medium heat for about 10 minutes or until the carrot is tender.

Bring another large pan of salted water to the boil, add the pasta and cook until *al dente*. Drain and set aside.

Add the beans and rosemary to the simmering vegetables and cook for a further 5 minutes or until the beans are just tender.

Meanwhile, in a smaller pan, gently heat the remaining garlic in the olive oil over a medium–low heat for just a few moments, without allowing it to brown.

Stir the pasta into the soup, then the garlicky oil, season to taste and serve right away.

Crema di Asparagi con Ravioli
Asparagus Soup with Ravioli

A bright-green purée of asparagus with ravioli or gnocchi floating in it and scented with nutmeg and chervil, this soup was inspired by a recent visit to Umbria. It's almost wicked in its seductive qualities.

SERVES 4

5 shallots, finely chopped
50g (2oz) butter
3 cloves garlic, finely chopped
2–3 tablespoons plain flour
1 litre (1¾ pints) hot chicken or vegetable stock
2 bundles of asparagus, sliced, reserving the tips and discarding the tough
    ends
5–6 tablespoons crème fraîche
Nutmeg for grating
Salt and freshly ground black pepper
Ravioli, tortellini or gnocchi, 3–4 per person
3–5 tablespoons freshly grated Parmesan cheese or similar
3–4 tablespoons freshly chopped chervil

Lightly sauté the shallots in 40g (1½ oz) of the butter in a large pan until they have softened, then add the garlic and cook for a few moments more. Stir in the flour and cook until lightly golden, then remove from the heat and pour in the stock all at once.

Return to the heat and cook, stirring continuously, until the mixture has thickened, then add the sliced asparagus (reserving the tips). Simmer until the asparagus is just cooked, then purée in a blender or food processor. Return to the pan, add the crème fraîche, season to taste with grated nutmeg, salt and pepper and set aside.

Cook the pasta in a large pan of rapidly boiling salted water until *al dente*, then drain.

Reheat the soup adding the reserved asparagus tips so that they cook until just tender and are still bright green, then add the pasta. Serve each bowl of soup with a dab of the remaining butter and a generous sprinkling of cheese and chervil.

Minestra con Aglio e Salvia

Garlic and Sage Soup with Pastina

The scent of garlic and sage permeates this comforting light soup. Eat it when you have a cold or flu, when you have only a few minutes to make supper, or whenever you feel like a perk-me-up. The perfect choice, too, for entertaining fellow 'agliophiles' (garlic-lovers).
SERVES 4

15 cloves garlic
1.5 litres (2¾ pints) chicken or vegetable stock
Several sprigs of fresh sage leaves
Pinch of salt
Pinch of cayenne pepper
2–3 tablespoons extra virgin olive oil
100g (4 oz) pastina (tiny pasta for soup)
1 egg and 1 egg yolk, lightly beaten
6 tablespoons or more freshly grated Parmesan cheese

Cut 10 of the garlic cloves into quarters or chunks and put them in a large pan with the stock and sage. Bring to the boil, then reduce the heat and simmer over a medium–low heat for about 10 minutes or until the garlic has softened.

Meanwhile, crush the remaining garlic with a large pinch of salt and cayenne pepper to a paste in a bowl (crushing the garlic brings out a stronger and nicer side to the garlic than a food processor would), stir in the olive oil and set aside.

Add the pastina to the simmering stock and cook for about 5 minutes, stirring so that it doesn't form lumps.

Slowly pour about 75ml (2½ fl oz) of the hot stock into the beaten egg, stirring continuously so that it doesn't cook or curdle. Then combine this mixture with the cheese before stirring it into the hot soup, cooking over a low heat for a few moments, or long enough to cook the eggs (but not scramble them) and thicken the soup.

Just before serving, stir in the garlic and olive oil paste – then eat up.

Zuppa di Vongole e Fregula
Soup of Clams and Tiny Pasta

Tiny pasta cooked in a fishy stock, along with a pan full of clams. The sun-dried tomatoes add punch, as does a dash of lemon. Fregula is a Sardinian couscous-like pasta.
SERVES 4–6

5 cloves garlic, finely chopped
2 tablespoons extra virgin olive oil
1 kg (2¼ lb) tiny clams, or a variety of sizes, cleaned
250ml (9 fl oz) dry white wine
Pinch of crumbled dried chilli
Large pinch or two of dried oregano leaves
2 litres (3½ pints) chicken/fish stock or half water and half stock
3–4 sun-dried tomatoes, cut or broken up into tiny pieces
3 tablespoons tomato purée or sun-dried tomato paste
200g (7 oz) tiny pasta shapes such as fregula, orzo, chicchi di pepe, or
    similar (see pages 11-12)
Freshly chopped parsley, as desired
½ lemon for squeezing

In a large heavy frying pan, heat the garlic and olive oil together with the clams. Cover and cook over a medium heat until the clams pop open, about 5 minutes. Discard any clams that have not opened by then.

Remove the clams from the pan and pour in the wine. Simmer with the clam juices until the liquid has reduced by about half, then add the chilli, oregano, stock, sun-dried tomatoes and tomato purée. Simmer together for 5 minutes or so to blend the flavours, then add the pasta and cook until *al dente*.

Return the clams and their juices to the pan, warm through, then serve big steamy bowls of the soup, sprinkled with parsley and a dash of lemon juice.

Minestrone Verde alla Genovese
Green Pesto Minestrone

Pesto is what makes this minestrone soup Genovese – a luscious, fragrant green purée of basil and garlic, stirred in at the last minute, turning a good soup into one that is sublime. I always think of eating this in the old city of Genoa and just the thought of it lifts my spirits every time.

Serve hot in warmed bowls on a chilly night to warm your bones, or cool on a sweltering day to fan your spirit.

SERVES 4

100g (4 oz) ditalini (little fingers) or other small soup pasta
2 tablespoons extra virgin olive oil
2 cloves garlic, finely chopped
1 leek, thinly sliced
1 litre (1¾ pints) vegetable stock
3–4 small new potatoes, scrubbed and diced
2–3 cabbage leaves, or ¼ green or white cabbage, thinly sliced
5 ripe fresh or canned tomatoes, diced (with their juices)
2 courgettes, diced
100–150g (4–5 oz) cooked fresh or frozen spinach, cut into strips or
    coarsely chopped
Handful of thin green beans, cut into bite-sized pieces
350–400g (12–14 oz) canned cannellini beans, drained
4 heaped tablespoons pesto (*see page 19*), or as desired
Freshly grated Parmesan cheese, as desired

Cook the pasta in a large pan of rapidly boiling salted water until just *al dente*. Drain, rinse in cold water and leave to cool while you prepare the soup.

Heat the oil in another large pan and sauté the garlic and leek until they begin to soften, about 5–8 minutes, then add the vegetable stock, new potatoes, cabbage and tomatoes. Simmer over a medium heat for 10–15 minutes or until the vegetables are almost tender. Add the courgettes and continue to cook for a further 5–10 minutes until tender, then add the spinach, green beans and cannellini beans. Continue to simmer until the green beans are bright green and just tender but still crisp. Stir in the pasta, and warm through briefly.

Ladle the soup into warmed soup bowls and place a spoonful of pesto in each, then sprinkle grated Parmesan over the top to taste.

Minestra di Zucchine

Courgette Soup with Pasta, White Wine and Fresh Herbs

If either golden courgettes or summer squash are available, use a mixture of half green and half golden. This light and lovely soup is a great way to enjoy your summer garden.

SERVES 4

1.5 litres (2¾ pints) chicken or vegetable stock
150ml (5 fl oz) dry white wine
2 teaspoons freshly chopped rosemary
1 teaspoon freshly chopped marjoram or thyme
450g (1 lb) young courgettes, cut into large bite-sized chunks
Salt and freshly ground black pepper
100g (4 oz) large chunky pasta such as conchiglie, rigatoni or penne
3 cloves garlic, chopped
2 tablespoons extra virgin olive oil
Pinch of crumbled dried chilli
2–3 tablespoons thinly shredded fresh basil leaves
Freshly grated Parmesan or pecorino romano cheese

Place the stock, wine, rosemary, marjoram or thyme and courgettes in a large pan and bring to the boil. Reduce the heat and simmer, covered, for about 15 minutes or until the courgettes are very tender. Season to taste with salt and pepper.

Meanwhile, in another large pan cook the pasta in rapidly boiling salted water until *al dente*, then drain and set aside.

Heat the garlic in the olive oil in a smaller pan until just fragrant but don't allow it to brown. Sprinkle in the chilli and warm through, then add this mixture to the soup.

Divide the pasta between bowls and ladle the soup over the top, generously sprinkled with the basil and cheese. Eat immediately.

Pasta Mista e Lenticchie
Pasta with Lentils

This earthy, rustic potful is part of the family of soupy pasta and pulse stews, much like pasta e fagioli. Pasta mista is a mix of many different types of pasta. The leftovers from various packets are kept together in a jar and, when there is enough, they are used to make soups such as this one. The lentils cook until just tender, the pasta absorbs the flavourful liquid, and a hit of garlicky oil is added at the end. An Italian friend says that whenever she visits her family's village she doesn't feel as if she's truly home until she sits down to a bowlful of this.

SERVES 4–6

250g (9 oz) green or brown lentils such as Castelluccio of Umbria or Puy
1 litre (1¾ pints) water
1 litre (1¾ pints) vegetable stock
3 cloves garlic, finely chopped
4 tablespoons or more extra virgin olive oil
Pinch of crumbled dried chilli
350g (12 oz) fresh or canned tomatoes
400g (14 oz) pasta mista
1–2 tablespoons freshly chopped parsley

Cook the lentils in the water in a large pan until they are tender, then add the stock. Set aside and keep warm.

Mix the garlic with the olive oil in a small bowl, then transfer about half to another bowl with the chilli and set aside.

Heat the garlic and olive oil in a large frying pan and cook the tomatoes over a medium heat for about 10 minutes. Tip this sauce into the lentils and stock and bring to the boil, then add the pasta. Simmer over a medium heat, stirring every so often, until the pasta is just tender, adding more stock as needed to keep the mixture soupy.

Serve in bowls with the garlic and chilli-flavoured oil swirled in at the last moment and sprinkled with parsley.

Pasta e Fagioli

Pasta and Bean Soup

Hearty fare, simple and delicious, eaten all over Italy – particularly in the south – and by Italians all over the world. Pink beans such as borlotti or pinto are simmered until soft, then the pasta is cooked in their juices. You can make this soup with canned beans, but it is more delicious with dried beans.

SERVES 4–6

250g (9 oz) dried borlotti, cranberry or pinto beans
Several sprigs of fresh rosemary
4 cloves garlic, finely chopped
5–6 tablespoons extra virgin olive oil
3 tablespoons tomato purée
Salt and freshly ground black pepper
350g (12 oz) small pasta such as ditalini (little fingers), elbows or
    conchiglie (shells)
4 slices prosciutto, cut into thin shreds (optional)
Freshly grated Parmesan cheese, to taste

Place the beans in a large saucepan with enough water to cover by at least 10cm (4 in). Bring to the boil, cook for 5 minutes then remove from the heat, cover and leave to sit for about 30 minutes. Drain, return the beans to the pan with a sprig of rosemary and pour over 1.5 litres (2¾ pints) fresh water. Bring to the boil, reduce the heat and simmer until the beans are tender, about 1½ hours, depending on the age and size of the beans. If they dry out too soon, add more water.

Meanwhile, combine the garlic with the olive oil in a small bowl and set aside to infuse.

When the beans are cooked, add the remaining rosemary to the pan with the tomato purée, seasoning and pasta and cook over a high heat until the pasta is tender, about 10 minutes, adding more liquid if needed. Remove from the heat and stir in the prosciutto, if using, and garlicky olive oil. The mixture should be thick and slightly soupy.

Serve in bowls, sprinkled with Parmesan.

Pasta e Ceci

Chickpea Soup with Fettuccine

Oh, so hearty and warming, so easy and quick too. And the fragrance – pure garlic wafting through your house with a whiff of rosemary here and there. You also have the thrilling sting of chilli, depending on how much you add.

If there are only two of you, the recipe can easily be halved, or you can have enough for tonight's supper and tomorrow's, too.

SERVES 4

700–800g (1½–1¾ lb) canned chickpeas, drained
1.5 litres (2¾ pints) vegetable or chicken stock
1–2 tablespoons finely chopped fresh rosemary
Large pinch or two of dried Italian mixed herbs, or similar
6 tablespoons extra virgin olive oil, plus extra for drizzling
10 cloves garlic, thinly sliced or coarsely chopped
Large pinch or two of crumbled dried chilli
4 medium-sized tomatoes, coarsely chopped
250g (9 oz) fettuccine (flat long ribbons)
2 tablespoons tomato purée
Salt and freshly ground black pepper
4 tablespoons freshly grated Parmesan cheese, or to taste

Purée the chickpeas in a food processor or blender with half the stock, half the rosemary and the dried herbs until very smooth, and set aside.

In a large heavy saucepan, gently heat the olive oil with the garlic and chilli until the garlic is fragrant and slightly golden but not browned, then add the tomatoes and cook over a high heat for a few more minutes.

Add the remaining stock and rosemary to the pan, along with the chickpea purée. Bring to the boil, then add the fettuccine and tomato purée, stir well, and simmer, stirring, until the pasta is cooked through. Season to taste.

Serve each bowlful with a tablespoon of Parmesan sprinkled on top and a drizzle of olive oil.

Pasta from the Garden

From the garden or the market, fresh and colourful vegetables combine brilliantly with pasta. Indeed, in any of their many wide and varied guises, a dish of pasta and vegetables is the standby of the Italian table, keeping the country going meal after meal, day by day – healthy, quick and delicious. Even if the sauce includes a little meat, or is based on fish, it is often the flavourful vegetables that star.

Italians live by the seasons – a fact strongly reflected in the pasta bowl. Sometimes the freshly picked vegetables will be simply boiled along with the pasta in the same pan, imparting their delicate flavours to each other. In spring, asparagus, peas or baby squash are each magical ingredients in their own right; and in summer it is the heady mix of aubergine, peppers and tomatoes which predominates. In autumn, tomatoes still reign supreme and are joined by pumpkin, onions and potatoes. During the colder months, cabbage and beans each contribute to wholesome winter-warming dishes.

All year round, herbs, fresh or dried, are crushed and simmered into sauces, ground down into an aromatic pesto, or torn and tossed on top, infusing their fragrance into pasta dishes and making meals that will never be forgotten…

Pasta di Ferragosto

Pasta for a Hot Summer's Day

Ripe summer tomatoes make the best raw sauce, but they sometimes appreciate the oomph of some tomato purée, especially in winter!

With no cooking involved, all you have to do is grate the tomatoes to create a light and refreshing sauce. Despite my passion for garlic, I have kept it out of the pot to allow the sheer unadulterated flavour of tomato, olive oil and basil to shine through. And if it's too hot for boiling pasta, the sauce makes a fabulous topping for bruschetta.

SERVES 4

8–10 ripe summer tomatoes
1–3 tablespoons tomato purée
3–5 tablespoons extra virgin olive oil
Sea salt and freshly ground black pepper
2–3 tablespoons very thinly sliced fresh basil
450g (1 lb) penne (quills) or other tubular pasta

Grate the tomatoes over a bowl on the large holes of a grater. Set them aside, including their juices. Add the tomato purée, olive oil, some sea salt and the basil and mix well.

Cook the pasta in a large pan of rapidly boiling salted water until *al dente*, then drain, saving a tablespoon or two of the cooking water for the sauce.

Combine the pasta with the sauce and reserved cooking water. Check the seasoning and serve.

Fettuccine Boscaiole

Fettuccine with Mushrooms and Truffle Oil

This dish was presented to me in a restaurant outside Siena, buried under a pile of freshly grated white truffles, foraged from the forest. However, truffle oil, or cheese preserved in truffle oil, makes a fine substitute. A few drops is enough to imbue a dish with the deliciously strong and provocative scent of truffles. But don't spill any on yourself and go near pigs – I've made this mistake…

Use whatever mushrooms are available – cultivated ones will be perked up by the dried wild ones.

SERVES 6

20g (¾ oz) dried porcini
3–4 dried morel mushrooms
250ml (9 fl oz) boiling vegetable or chicken stock
40g (1½ oz) butter
5 shallots, finely chopped
3 cloves garlic, finely chopped
100–150g (4–5 oz) fresh mushrooms such as oyster, shiitake, trompettes
    de mort (horn of plenty), or common cultivated ones, thinly sliced
3 tablespoons extra virgin olive oil
4–6 ripe medium-sized tomatoes, diced, or 1 carton of cherry tomatoes,
    halved
½ teaspoon freshly chopped rosemary, or a mixture of rosemary and
    flat-leaf parsley
Salt
Small pinch of sugar
250ml (9 fl oz) dry white wine
4 tablespoons pesto (*see page 19*)
350g (12 oz) good-quality egg fettuccine
Truffle oil

Place the dried mushrooms in a bowl or saucepan and pour the boiling stock over them. Cover and let them soak for about 30 minutes to rehydrate them. Remove them from the soaking liquid using a slotted spoon and squeeze them over a bowl so that none of the intensely flavoured juices are wasted. Cut the porcini into bite-sized pieces and the morels into halves or quarters, and set them aside.

In a large frying pan, melt the butter and lightly sauté the shallots and half the garlic until soft. Add the sliced fresh mushrooms and cook for a few minutes until they are just tender. Stir in the rehydrated mushrooms and cook together for a few more minutes. Spoon all the mushrooms into a dish and set aside. Strain the mushroom-infused stock through a cheesecloth or a fine sieve into the pan and allow it to simmer over a medium–high heat until it's reduced to a few tablespoons of intensely flavoured sauce. Pour this over the mushrooms.

Heat a tablespoon of the olive oil in the same pan and cook the tomatoes over a high heat until they are warmed through and slightly cooked – they mustn't get mushy. Stir in the remaining garlic with the rosemary, a pinch each of salt and sugar and cook for a few minutes more. Transfer the tomatoes to the dish of mushrooms. Pour the wine into the pan and boil it down until it's reduced to only a few tablespoons then add it to the mushrooms and tomatoes.

Mix the pesto with the remaining olive oil, then smear it around the edge of each person's plate or one large serving platter.

Meanwhile, cook the pasta in a large pan of rapidly boiling salted water until *al dente*. Drain and reserve a little of the cooking water. Toss the hot pasta with the mushroom and tomato sauce, adding a few spoonfuls of the cooking water for extra moisture. Sprinkle generously with truffle oil.

Heap a portion of the pasta in the centre of each pesto-smeared plate or tip it all on to the large platter and serve right away.

Gemelli alla Caprese

Pasta Twists with Cherry Tomatoes, Mozzarella, and Basil

Ripe, sweet, juicy tomatoes, milky soft mozzarella cheese and sweet, fresh basil tangled around chewy twists of pasta. It is the exquisite taste of summer, conjuring up sizzling days and balmy nights on the isle of Capri. It is also everything a good pasta dish should be: tangy, savoury, ultra satisfying and yet not heavy. Be as lavish as you can with the basil; its herby fragrance makes this dish special.
SERVES 4–6

100ml (4 fl oz) extra virgin olive oil
2–3 cloves garlic, finely chopped or crushed
250–300g (9–11 oz) ripe cherry tomatoes, halved
100ml (4 fl oz) crushed tomatoes (passata or puréed canned tomatoes with
    their juices), or 1–2 tablespoons tomato purée
Salt and freshly ground black pepper
400g (14 oz) gemelli (chunky pasta twists)
1 medium bunch (about 3 handfuls) fresh basil leaves, roughly torn
Pinch of sugar, if needed
50g (2 oz) Parmesan cheese, freshly grated, or as desired
175–200g (6–7 oz) fresh mozzarella, diced

Heat the olive oil in a large pan and gently fry the garlic until golden but not brown. Add the tomatoes and allow them to sizzle in the garlic oil before stirring in the crushed tomatoes. Cook for 5–10 minutes, shaking the pan every so often to prevent the sauce from sticking and burning.

Bring a large pan of salted water to the boil and simmer the gemelli until *al dente*. Then transfer a small ladleful (a few tablespoons) of the pasta cooking water to the simmering tomato sauce, along with half the basil. Drain the pasta and season the sauce with salt, pepper and a pinch of sugar if needed.

Toss the pasta with the sauce, stir in the Parmesan, then fork the mozzarella dice gently through the mixture. But be careful not to toss the mozzarella about too enthusiastically, as it will form one large lump in the middle.

Serve right away, scattering the rest of the basil on top.

Strangozzi al Limone
Fat Spaghetti with Bay-scented Lemon Sauce

Refreshing lemon sauces are considered chic throughout Italy. My Sardinian friend Paolo Ardisson, a London olive-oil importer, tosses pasta in just lemon juice and grated zest along with his beautiful olive oil. I've added a slosh of wine and bay leaves and serve it with strangozzi, for its satisfying chunky yet spaghetti-like feel.

Potato cooked with the pasta gives the sauce a creamy texture and balances the acidity of the lemon. For less of a tang, reduce the lemon juice but not the zest.

SERVES 4–6

1 large or 2 medium-sized potatoes, peeled and diced
Salt and freshly ground black pepper
4–6 tablespoons extra virgin olive oil
1 onion, chopped
3 cloves garlic, coarsely chopped
½ lemon, rind included, sliced crosswise
2–3 bay leaves
125ml (4½ fl oz) dry white wine
Grated zest and juice of 2½ lemons
350g (12 oz) strangozzi (fat spaghetti)
4–6 tablespoons grated Parmesan cheese

Bring a large pan of salted water to the boil and cook the potatoes while you make the sauce.

In a frying pan, gently heat half the olive oil and sauté the onion until softened. Add the garlic and lemon slices, cook a few moments, then add the bay leaves and pour in the wine. Bring to the boil and cook until the liquid is reduced to about 4 tablespoons. Remove the bay leaves and add the lemon zest and juice and the remaining olive oil. Remove from the heat.

Add the pasta to the potatoes in the water and cook until just tender, about 10 minutes. Drain lightly, leaving in some of the water, then toss the pasta and potatoes with the onion mixture and Parmesan. Mix well and serve right away.

Pasta con Pomodori Arrostiti

Pasta with Roasted-tomato Sauce

Roast a pan of summer's ripe and aromatic tomatoes, squeeze them out of their skins with their intensely flavoured juices, add olive oil, garlic and basil, and you have a delicious basic sauce. Even watery winter tomatoes are good this way, enriched with tomato purée.

Any type of pasta can be used: I like slippery long strands of spaghetti or the thinner spaghettini – it's so light and feels playful in the mouth, cloaked in the sun-drenched flavour of the tomatoes.

SERVES 4

About 24 small–to–medium tomatoes
Salt and freshly ground black pepper
Sugar for sprinkling
6 tablespoons extra virgin olive oil
8 cloves garlic, unpeeled
1–3 tablespoons tomato purée (optional)
400g (14 oz) spaghetti
Large handful of basil, roughly torn
Freshly grated pecorino or Parmesan cheese, to taste

Preheat the oven to 180°C/350°F/Gas 4.

Cut half of the tomatoes in half, leaving the remainder whole, and arrange them all in a large shallow baking dish. Sprinkle generously with salt and very lightly with sugar, then drizzle with the olive oil. Place them under a hot grill until their skins begin to char, about 10–15 minutes, then remove the dish to the oven with the garlic cloves and bake for 35–40 minutes or until the tomatoes are slightly shrunken, their skins have popped and shrivelled and their juices have reduced a little.

When the tomatoes are cool enough to handle – and this is best done up to a day in advance, so that their juices have a chance to thicken slightly and concentrate in flavour – with clean hands, remove their skins and squeeze out the flesh and juice into a bowl. Squeeze the garlic cloves into the same bowl, and mash it all together with a fork. Check the seasoning and, if more oomph is needed, stir in tomato purée to taste.

Meanwhile, cook the spaghetti in a large pan of rapidly boiling salted water until *al dente*. Drain and serve tossed with the sauce, sprinkled with basil and grated cheese.

Six Variations of Pasta with Roasted-tomato Sauce

Pasta with Roasted-tomato Sauce *(see page 53) is a great basic recipe, which you can tart up in numerous different ways. Use 400g (14 oz) of pasta for each one (to serve 4) and cook in a large pan of rapidly boiling salted water until* al dente. *Drain and serve tossed with any of the following:*

Bucatini con Melanzane e Pomodori Arrosto
Bucatini with Aubergine and Roasted-tomato Sauce

SERVES 4

A variation on the Catanese *Pasta alla Norma (see page 74)*. Thinly slice an aubergine crosswise and lightly brown each side in several tablespoons of extra virgin olive oil in a heavy frying pan. Toss the drained bucatini in the roasted-tomato sauce and heap in the centre of a dish with the aubergine slices around it. Sprinkle an aged salty pecorino or ricotta cheese over the top if you have some – a combination of freshly grated feta and Parmesan cheese if you don't.

Penne con Fagiolini, Olive e Pomodori Arrosto
Penne with Green Beans, Olives and Roasted-tomato Sauce

SERVES 4

Cook the penne in a large pan of rapidly boiling salted water until about 5 minutes before it is ready, then add 200g (7 oz) thin, fine green beans, topped and tailed and cut into bite-sized pieces. Continue to boil until the pasta is *al dente* and the beans are just tender. Drain and toss with the roasted-tomato sauce and about 15 stoned and quartered, oil-cured black olives. Sprinkle with roughly torn fresh basil leaves and freshly grated Parmesan cheese and serve.

Capelli d'Angelo con Gamberi e Pomodori Arrosto
Angel Hair Pasta with Prawns and Roasted-tomato Sauce

SERVES 4

Lightly sauté 350g (12 oz) shelled prawns in a little extra virgin olive oil until they just colour. Toss the drained pasta with the roasted-tomato sauce and prawns. Serve garnished with a large handful of roughly torn fresh basil, but no cheese.

Penne con Peperoni, Finocchi e Pomodori Arrosto
Penne with Roasted Peppers, Fennel and Roasted-tomato Sauce

SERVES 4

Cut 1 red and 1 yellow pepper into quarters, seed, and arrange them in a roasting pan along with 2 bulbs of fennel cut into wedges or quarters. Drizzle with olive oil and roast in the oven at the same time as the tomatoes, for 35–40 minutes, or until soft. Remove from the oven, chop the fennel, skin and dice the peppers, then toss with the cooked and drained penne, roasted-tomato sauce and some roughly torn fresh basil. Sprinkle with freshly grated Parmesan cheese before serving.

Spaghetti con Pomodori Arrosto e Broccoli alla Campagnola
Spaghetti with Roasted-tomato Sauce and Broccoli

SERVES 4

When cooking the spaghetti add a head of broccoli or cauliflower, broken up into florets, to the pan during the last 5 minutes or so. Broccoli will only take a few minutes to cook, cauliflower a few minutes longer. When the vegetables are just tender and the spaghetti *al dente*, drain, reserving a little of the cooking liquid. Toss the spaghetti and broccoli or cauliflower with the roasted-tomato sauce, moistening it all with 2–3 tablespoons of olive oil and a little bit of the cooking liquid, then toss in a handful each of pine nuts and raisins, and a pinch of crumbled dried chilli to taste. You could also add some meatballs to this recipe.

Gemelli con Pomodori Arrosto, Gorgonzola e Basilico
Gemelli with Roasted-tomato Sauce, Blue Cheese and Basil

SERVES 4

Toss the roasted-tomato sauce with the cooked and drained gemelli or other chewy pasta twists. Before serving, crumble in about 125g (4½ oz) Gorgonzola or other blue cheese and several tablespoons or a small bunch of roughly torn fresh basil.

Penne al Limone e Peperoncino
Penne with Lemon and Chilli

Tangy and invigorating with a hit of hot chilli and lemon, this is great to whip up at a moment's notice – I always keep a jar of dried breadcrumbs in La Dispensa *(see page 20) for such emergencies.*

SERVES 4–6

2–3 tablespoons capers, rinsed if preserved in vinegar, soaked and drained
    if preserved in salt
15 cloves garlic, coarsely chopped
Several pinches of crumbled dried chilli
125ml (4½ fl oz) extra virgin olive oil
450g (1 lb) penne
Grated zest and juice of 1 lemon
3–4 tablespoons dried breadcrumbs
Salt

Gently heat the capers, garlic and chilli in a heavy frying pan with the olive oil until the garlic turns lightly golden. Set aside.

Bring a large pan of salted water to a rapid boil and cook the penne until *al dente*. Drain, reserving a few spoonfuls of the cooking water, and toss into the garlic-flavoured oil, mixing well. Add a spoonful or two of the cooking liquid, the lemon zest and juice. Return to a high heat, toss in the breadcrumbs and check the seasoning – you may not need any black pepper. Serve right away.

Trofie o Trenette al Pesto
The Real Pasta with Pesto

Traditional pasta al pesto in Liguria is prepared with either chunky trofie, or with flat ribbons of trenette or tagliatelle. Sometimes you'll find pesto on fazzoletti, silky 'handkerchiefs' of pasta, or delicate, melting gnocchi.

Diced potato added to the pasta cooking water helps the pesto cling to the pasta, and a handful of fresh thin green beans adds freshness and crispness to what can be a rich dish. Sometimes olive oil is offered at the table to sprinkle over the dish instead of Parmesan.

SERVES 4

1 large baking potato, peeled and diced
Salt
250g (9 oz) thin green beans, cut into bite-sized pieces
350g–400g (12–14 oz) trofie, trenette, tagliatelle, or other pasta as
    described above
1 recipe pesto (*see page 19*)
Freshly grated Parmesan cheese and/or olive oil for serving

Bring a large pan of salted water to the boil and cook the potato until almost tender. Add the beans and pasta, return the water to the boil and cook for another 5–6 minutes, until the pasta is *al dente* and the beans are bright green. Drain, reserving a few spoonfuls of the cooking water. Toss the pasta and beans with the pesto, adding as much of the reserved cooking water as needed. Serve sprinkled with the cheese and/or olive oil.

Orecchiette con Broccoli

Little Ears with Broccoli Sauce

I once ate this dish at a 'slow food' ristorante in the old part of Ostuni, a Moorish-looking town in Puglia – the heel end of Italy's 'boot' – sitting on a hillside above endless olive groves. It is the local speciality and the broccoli is cooked until it becomes a mushy sauce for the pasta. Use broccoli that's green and fresh and bursting with flavour, especially the Roman variety, with the pointed head and strangely patterned florets – it's just so good.
SERVES 4–6

800g (1¾ lb) broccoli, the stems trimmed and peeled, the whole bunch
    coarsely chopped
Salt and freshly ground black pepper
125ml (4½ fl oz) extra virgin olive oil
6–10 cloves garlic, sliced
About ⅛–¼ teaspoon or more crumbled dried chilli
450g (1 lb) orecchiette (flat ear-shaped discs)
Handful of freshly grated Parmesan or pecorino cheese

Bring a large pan of salted water to the boil and cook the broccoli until *al dente*. Remove from the heat and fish the broccoli out with a strainer or slotted spoon, reserving the water for the pasta.

In a heavy frying pan, large enough to hold all the broccoli, heat the olive oil and gently cook the garlic in it for a moment or two, until just turning golden. Add the chilli and broccoli, with a ladleful or so of the broccoli cooking water, and cover the pan. Cook over a medium–high heat, stirring and adding more water from time to time. It needs to become quite soft, almost a chunky purée. If the mixture is too sloppy, remove the cover and continue to cook over a high heat until the liquid evaporates. Season to taste and set aside while you cook the pasta.

Bring the remaining reserved broccoli water to the boil and cook the orecchiette until *al dente*, then drain lightly, saving a few spoonfuls of the cooking water. Toss the orecchiette with the broccoli sauce and a spoonful or two of the cooking water, then sprinkle on a handful of the Parmesan. Serve right away.

Tagliatelle alle Erbe
Garlicky Tagliatelle with Fresh Herbs

Heaps of chopped herbs, warmed through with garlicky olive oil then flung into a bowl of green-flecked noodles – comforting, fresh and aromatic. Tear the herbs with your hands, crush them between your fingers and fling them on to the plate. Not only will you bring out their fragrance, but it's a good stress-reducing exercise, too! Replace the olive oil with butter for a delicate, buttery pasta and for extra panache, scatter purple chive flowers over the top.

SERVES 4–6

8 cloves garlic, chopped
100–125ml (4–4½ fl oz) extra virgin olive oil
6 tablespoons chopped, crushed or roughly torn fresh herbs such as sweet basil, chives or parsley
450g (1 lb) tagliatelle (thin flat ribbons)
Salt and freshly ground black pepper

In a large pan, warm the garlic in the olive oil for just a moment, until it smells beautiful, then toss all the herbs in and remove from the heat. Set aside while you cook the pasta in a large pan of rapidly boiling salted water until *al dente*. Drain, reserving a spoonful or two of the hot cooking water. Toss the pasta into the herbed oil and stir in the reserved water. Season to taste and serve.

Spaghetti agli Spinaci
Spaghetti with Spinach, Lemon and Pancetta

So easy to throw together, this is perfect summer fare: fresh, leafy greens, tangy lemons and a nip of pancetta. It is uncomplicated and light and a good reason to always have a little pancetta in the house.
SERVES 4

1–2 lemons, unwaxed and preferably organic
125g (4½ oz) pancetta, diced
3 tablespoons extra virgin olive oil
6 spring onions, thinly sliced
225g (8 oz) fresh spinach, sliced
5 cloves garlic, chopped
Salt and coarsely ground black pepper
450g (1 lb) spaghetti
50–100g (2–4 oz) Parmesan cheese, freshly grated, or as desired

Zest about half to a whole lemon into a small bowl, using either a zester (which I heartily recommend) or a grater. Squeeze the juice from one or both lemons (if using) into another small bowl and set aside.

Heat a large frying pan and sauté the pancetta until the fat runs and it's lightly browned. If there is not enough fat, add a little of the olive oil. Add the spring onions, remaining olive oil and spinach and cook, stirring, for a few minutes until a sauce forms (the spinach will give off lots of liquid). Stir in the garlic, continue to cook for a few moments and set aside.

In a large pan of rapidly boiling salted water, cook the spaghetti until *al dente*, then drain, reserving a little of the cooking water. Toss the hot pasta with the spinach mixture, some of the cooking water if needed, lemon zest and juice and most of the Parmesan, and season to taste.

Serve up steaming hot, with an extra flurry of Parmesan on top.

Caserecci con Pesto Trapanese

Fat Pasta Twists with Sicilian-style Pesto Sauce

Unlike the basil pesto of Liguria (see page 19), the main ingredient in Sicily's Trapanese pesto is tomatoes. It is also about almonds: traditionally this is a summer dish with fresh ripe tomatoes and sweet basil, blended with young and tender almonds. These days dried almonds are used year-round, and they are not only fine – I like toasted ones, too – but they give a very different yet delicious result. Chewy, squat pasta twists, penne, spaghettini or flat linguine all go well with this sauce.
SERVES 4

2–3 cloves garlic, finely chopped
30g (1 oz) shelled almonds, raw or roasted, coarsely chopped
85g (3½ oz) Parmesan or pecorino cheese, freshly grated or in small pieces
30–40g (1–1½ oz) fresh basil leaves
125ml (4½ fl oz) extra virgin olive oil
100g (4 oz) fresh ripe tomatoes, diced
Salt and freshly ground black pepper
400g (14 oz) caserecci, gemelli (pasta twists), or similar
Extra Parmesan for grating on top

If preparing by hand, chop everything finely and mix together in a bowl. If using a food processor or blender, whizz the garlic, then add the almonds and cheese and process until the almonds are chunky. Remove to a bowl and finely chop the basil in the processor or blender, then add the olive oil and whizz together. Stir this into the nut and cheese mixture, then stir in the tomatoes and taste for seasoning.

In a large pan of rapidly boiling salted water, cook the pasta until *al dente*, then drain, reserving a little of the cooking water. Toss the hot pasta with the pesto, adding a few tablespoons of the reserved water if and as desired. Serve, offering extra Parmesan to grate on top.

VARIATION

In the little Mediterranean island of Pantelleria, the locally grown capers are tossed into the mix, giving a tangy, briny quality to the finished dish. These capers are terrific, preserved in salt rather than vinegar (*see page 20*).

Farfalle con Pesto d'Invernale
Butterfly Pasta with Walnut Sauce

This creamy winter pesto made of walnuts and yogurt is a speciality of Liguria, the Riviera dei Fiori (Riviera of Flowers). Sit on a balcony, with the sea at your feet, and a plate of chunky pasta, such as trofie (see page 12), gnocchi, or spinach-stuffed ravioli slathered with walnut sauce, and you'll forget it is winter elsewhere.

Due to Liguria's connections to Sardinia and Sardinia's with Bulgaria, yogurt is a traditional ingredient in ancient pesto recipes. Some believe that a thick yogurt pounded with herbs might have been the first pesto.

SERVES 4

3 cloves garlic, chopped
100g (4 oz) walnut pieces
2 heaped tablespoons Greek yogurt or crème fraîche
60g (2½ oz) freshly grated Parmesan cheese (or diced Parmesan cheese, if using a food processor), plus extra for sprinkling
Several sprigs fresh thyme, stalks removed
6–8 tablespoons extra virgin olive oil
2–3 tablespoons or more of cold water
Salt and freshly ground black pepper
400g (14 oz) medium farfalle (butterflies)

In a food processor, chop the garlic, then add the walnut pieces and whizz until they are finely chopped. Add the yogurt, Parmesan and thyme, and whizz again, then slowly add the olive oil, allowing the mixture to thicken and emulsify. Still whirling, add the water, salt and pepper, then turn off the machine and taste for seasoning. The sauce should be thick and creamy, the consistency of a thinnish hummus.

Meanwhile, cook the pasta in a large pan of rapidly boiling salted water until just *al dente*. Drain, reserving a little of the cooking liquid. Toss the hot pasta quickly with the creamy walnut sauce and the cooking water to loosen it. Serve right away, with a sprinkling of extra Parmesan.

Pasta ai Funghi
Pasta with Porcini

Ah, porcini, those whimsical gifts from nature that transform the forests of Tuscany to a treasure trove and Florence's restaurant windows into still-life paintings.

While you cannot plan on fresh porcini being available when you want them, dried wild mushrooms are just as delicious; perhaps even more so, as drying concentrates their flavours and you can use the soaking liquid in the sauce.
SERVES 4–6

50g (2 oz) dried porcini
250ml (9 fl oz) very hot water, not boiling
30g (1oz) unsalted butter
5 shallots, finely chopped
2 cloves garlic, finely chopped
2–3 tablespoons brandy
250ml (9 fl oz) double cream or single cream
Nutmeg for grating
Salt and freshly ground black pepper
350g (12 oz) fresh fettuccine or pappardelle (long flat ribbons)
50–100g (2–4 oz) Parmesan cheese, freshly grated

Place the porcini in a bowl and cover with the hot water. Soak for 20 minutes or until they have softened and the liquid has cooled. Remove the porcini with a slotted spoon, reserving the liquid for the sauce, and cut them into bite-sized pieces or shreds.

Gently heat half the butter in a large frying pan and lightly sauté the shallots, garlic and porcini. Turn off the heat and carefully stir in the brandy, so that it doesn't burst into flames. Return the pan to the heat and cook on high until the liquid has almost evaporated. Strain the reserved porcini liquid into the pan through muslin, and simmer for a further 5–10 minutes or until it has reduced by about half. Stir in the cream, grate in as much nutmeg as desired, and season to taste. Set aside and keep warm.

Meanwhile, cook the pasta in a large pan of rapidly boiling salted water until *al dente*, drain and reserve a few spoonfuls of the cooking liquid. Toss the pasta with the sauce and cooking water, dot with the remaining butter and shower with Parmesan. Dish up in warm bowls.

Penne Rigate con Piselli e Funghi in Salsa Rossa

Pasta Quills with Peas and Mushrooms in Creamy Tomato Sauce

Salsa rossa, or creamy tomato sauce, so full of tomato flavour yet smoothed – caressed even – with cream, is one of Tuscany's most delicious and sensuous sauces, coming in many guises. Here we're saucing up penne rigate, as the peas and mushrooms hide so fetchingly inside the tubes and the sauce clings so tantalisingly to the outside ridges.

Sometimes I add several fresh ordinary mushrooms to the sauce, too – chopped and added to the onion along with the dried mushrooms.

SERVES 4

40g (1½ oz) butter
1 onion, finely chopped
1–2 cloves garlic, finely chopped
400g (14 oz) canned tomatoes, diced or crushed
150g (5 oz) frozen or young fresh blanched peas
A few leaves of fresh basil, roughly torn
5–10 slices dried porcini mushrooms (or a mixture of dried wild
    mushrooms), broken up
75ml (2½ fl oz) each of dry white wine and vegetable stock
175–200g (6–7 oz) crème fraîche or similar
Salt and freshly ground black pepper
500g (1 lb 3 oz) penne rigate (ridged quills)
8 tablespoons freshly grated Parmesan cheese

Melt the butter in a large frying pan and lightly sauté the onion until soft, then stir in the garlic, tomatoes, peas, basil, dried mushrooms, wine and stock. Bring to the boil, reduce the heat and leave the mixture to simmer and thicken until it has reduced by about half. Stir in the crème fraîche and season, then remove from the heat and keep warm.

Bring a large pan of salted water to a rapid boil and cook the pasta until *al dente*. Drain, reserving a few spoonfuls of the cooking water. Toss the hot pasta with the sauce, adding a few spoonfuls of the cooking water as you do so, then scatter 4–5 tablespoons of Parmesan over the top. Serve right away with the remaining Parmesan offered to those who would like more.

Spaghetti Tartufati con Asparagi e Uova

Truffled Spaghetti with Asparagus and Egg

This is excellent midnight-supper food – very satisfying, evoking a taste of the Tuscan countryside – which only takes about 10 minutes to prepare. A fried egg plopped on top of a bowl of spaghetti is very cucina povera, *food of the poor, as so much of Italy's wonderful food is. The asparagus cooks along with the pasta, imparting its flavour. Use a really good cheese: a mouthful of both asparagus and good Parmesan or pecorino is sublime.*

SERVES 4

350g (12 oz) spaghetti or spaghettini
1 large bunch asparagus, tough ends discarded, the stalks and tips cut into
    julienne
4 free-range, organic eggs
About 100g (4 oz) unsalted butter, or as desired
Salt and freshly ground black pepper
A generous shaking of truffle oil
100g (4 oz) or more good Parmesan or pecorino cheese, half grated, half
    finely shaved
Fresh black or white truffles (optional)

Place the spaghetti in a large pan of rapidly boiling salted water and after a few minutes add the asparagus. When the spaghetti is *al dente*, the asparagus will be tender. Drain lightly, saving some of the cooking liquid.

Meanwhile, fry the eggs in about half the butter.

Toss the pasta and asparagus with the remaining butter, adding more if needed. Season to taste, stirring in a little of the reserved cooking liquid, then mix in the truffle oil and grated cheese.

Serve each bowl of pasta topped with an egg and shavings of Parmesan. If, lucky you, fresh truffles are in your kitchen, shave a bit on to this fine dish and eat right away.

Insalata di Orzo, Zucchine e Rucola

Cool Pasta with Courgettes and Rocket

A cookery week in Puglia: it's too hot to think. We float as if in a dream through the oleanders to the long wooden tables around the open-air kitchen in an olive grove. We eat meals we have prepared with Marco Corsica, our chef: great tomatoey dishes, rich with local vegetables, and fish selected from the local catch.

This dish is my version of a salad Marco prepared for us – lemony and tomatoey, spiked with lush olive oil and peppery rocket.

SERVES 6

300g (11 oz) orzo or other small soup pasta
Salt and freshly ground black pepper
2 courgettes, diced
3 cloves garlic, finely chopped
150g (5 oz) cherry tomatoes, halved
50g (2 oz) rocket, coarsely chopped
Juice of 2 lemons
100ml (4 fl oz) extra virgin olive oil

Bring a large pan of salted water to the boil and cook the pasta on a high heat. After about 5 minutes, add the courgettes and boil together, until the pasta is *al dente* and the courgettes are cooked. Drain carefully.

Toss the pasta and courgettes with the garlic, tomatoes, rocket, lemon juice, olive oil, salt and pepper and leave to cool. Serve at room temperature.

VARIATION

Insalata di Pasta e Zucchine con Polpo
Cool Pasta with Courgettes and Baby Octopus

Cook 450g (1 lb) baby octopus, cleaned and cut into small pieces, in lightly salted simmering water with a wine cork in the water. I am not sure why we do this, but I just know that Marco never cooks octopus without it. Remove from the heat and tenderise the octopus by leaving it in the hot water to steep and cool. When the pasta and courgettes are cooked, toss in the cooled octopus with the rest of the ingredients.

Spaghetti ai Peperoncini Verdi
Spaghetti with Green Italian Peppers

In Campania, the area of Italy around Naples, lusty tomato and pepper sauces are everyday fare, simple in ingredients and lean in animal fats. No butter, no cheese, just lots of luscious olive oil and vegetables.
SERVES 4–6

200ml (7 fl oz) extra virgin olive oil
600–800g (1 lb 5 oz–1¾ lb) green Italian peppers or a combination of
    ordinary green peppers and one or two anaheim chillies
¼ fresh green chilli (not *too* hot), chopped (only use this if not using
    anaheims or other slightly hot peppers)
600–800g (1 lb 5 oz–1¾ lb) ripe fresh or canned tomatoes, chopped or
    quartered
4 cloves garlic, sliced
Salt and freshly ground black pepper
Pinch of sugar
10–15 leaves fresh basil, roughly torn
400g (14 oz) spaghetti

Heat the oil in a large frying pan and fry the whole peppers and chillies, covering the pan to keep it from splattering. After 5 minutes or so turn the peppers over, cover and cook and repeat until they are lightly browned all over. Remove them from the pan with a slotted spoon and leave to cool.

Add the tomatoes and garlic to the oil in the pan and cook over a medium high heat until the tomatoes have reduced in volume by at least a half and are thick and saucy. This will take about 15 minutes if using canned tomatoes, and about 25 minutes for fresh. At this stage you can purée the sauce in a blender or food processor or leave it chunky. Return the sauce to the pan and continue to simmer.

When the peppers are cool enough to handle, remove their skins if they seem thick and too blistered. Then remove the stems and seeds and slice the peppers up. Add them plus any juices to the simmering tomatoes. Season to taste, adding a pinch of sugar if needed, and stir in the basil. Cook for a further 10 minutes or so, just long enough to concentrate the sauce and combine the flavours.

Meanwhile, cook the pasta in a large pan of rapidly boiling salted water until *al dente* and drain, reserving some of the cooking liquid. Toss the drained pasta into the sauce, along with a few spoonfuls of the cooking liquid, and serve immediately.

Tortiglioni con Peperoni e Zucchine

Pasta Tubes with Mixed Peppers and Courgettes

Just the thing for summer: brightly coloured peppers, courgettes and tomatoes. If you had to conjure up the taste of a Mediterranean summer, this would be it. To gild the lily and oomph up the character of the dish, serve with a sharp fresh white cheese such as feta or quatirolo grated on top, or a handful of capers, or sweet ricotta cheese and grated pungent Parmesan or pecorino.

SERVES 4–6

1 each of red, yellow and green peppers, stems and seeds removed, cut into
  bite-sized pieces
1 onion, diced
3–4 tablespoons extra virgin olive oil
1 medium or 2 smallish courgettes, halved lengthwise and sliced thinly
5 cloves garlic, coarsely chopped
Salt and freshly ground black pepper
Large pinch of sugar
4–6 tablespoons passata or chunky tomato sauce
Pinch of crumbled dried chilli (optional)
Handful of fresh basil leaves, roughly torn
500g (1lb 3 oz) tortiglioni, or similar

Brown the peppers and onion in the olive oil in a heavy frying pan. When they are lightly browned in spots, push them to the side and brown the courgette. Add the garlic, salt, pepper and sugar and cook for a few minutes more. Stir in the passata, chilli, if using, and half the basil, and heat the sauce through. Set aside.

Cook the pasta in a large pan of rapidly boiling salted water until just *al dente*. Drain, reserving a little of the cooking water. Toss the hot pasta into the sauce, adding a few spoonfuls of the cooking water – just enough to bind it all together. Toss in the remaining basil and serve.

Pasta alla Norma

Sicilian Pasta with Aubergine

Although eaten throughout Sicily, it is in the composer Vincenzo Bellini's home town of Catania that Pasta alla Norma *is the most famous dish. When his opera* Norma *became a great 'hit' in 1831, the term 'alla Norma' became fashionable slang to describe anything that was really good – and was given to Catania's traditional dish of pasta with tomato sauce and aubergines.*

SERVES 4–6

Olive oil, about 125ml (4½ fl oz)
2 aubergines, cut crosswise, about 1 cm (½ in) thick
1 onion, finely chopped
3 cloves garlic, finely chopped
600g (1 lb 5 oz) fresh or canned chopped tomatoes
Salt and freshly ground black pepper
Pinch of sugar, to taste
400g (14 oz) spaghetti
2–3 tablespoons freshly torn basil leaves or fresh marjoram or oregano leaves
100g (4 oz) salted ricotta or other pungent fresh salty cheese such as feta, halloumi or pecorino, grated

In a large frying pan, heat some of the oil and fry the aubergine slices until they are crisp and browned on both sides, adding more oil when necessary. Remove and place on absorbent paper to drain.

To make the sauce, gently heat a tablespoon of the olive oil and lightly sauté the onion and garlic, then add the tomatoes. Season with salt, pepper and sugar to taste and simmer over a medium heat until the tomatoes have reduced to a flavourful sauce-like consistency. Purée the mixture in a blender, if you prefer a smooth sauce, and keep warm.

Cook the spaghetti in a large pan of rapidly boiling salted water until just *al dente*, then drain, reserving a few spoonfuls of the cooking liquid. Toss the spaghetti in the tomato sauce, then heap it on to a serving platter. Arrange the aubergine slices around the edge and sprinkle with the fresh herbs and cheese. Eat right away.

Pasta alla Siracusana

Pasta Wheels with Aubergine, Peppers, Capers, Olives and Tomatoes

From the Sicilian town of Syracuse, this is an almost puttanesca-type sauce. It's exuberant in flavour with capers, peppers and olives. A hint of saffron gives an exotic edge, or you could add a couple of chopped anchovies instead.
SERVES 4

1 large aubergine, or 2 small-to-medium aubergines, diced
3–4 tablespoons extra virgin olive oil
2 onions, finely chopped
5–6 cloves garlic, finely chopped
200ml (7 fl oz) dry white wine
2 red peppers, roasted and peeled
600g (1 lb 5 oz) canned chopped tomatoes, or half fresh ripe chopped
 tomatoes and half canned
3–4 tablespoons tomato purée
2 tablespoons capers, either in vinegar or, preferably, salted dried capers,
 soaked in cold water, then rinsed
Pinch of sugar
Salt and freshly ground black pepper
Pinch of saffron soaked in 3 tablespoons hot water
450g (1 lb) rotelle (little wheels), or penne (quills)
2 tablespoons black olive paste (*olivada*) or about 20 black olives, stoned
 and sliced or quartered
Freshly grated Parmesan or pecorino cheese, to taste

In a large frying pan, fry the aubergine in the olive oil over a medium-low to medium heat until browned and tender, then add the onion and half the garlic and sauté together until the onions are soft and golden. Pour in the wine, cook over a high heat until the liquid has been almost absorbed, then add the red peppers, tomatoes and tomato purée. Simmer over a medium heat for about 10 minutes.

Add the remaining garlic, capers, pinch of sugar if needed, salt, pepper, saffron and its liquid. Taste for seasoning, set aside and keep warm.

Cook the rotelle in a large pan of rapidly boiling salted water until *al dente,* then drain. Stir the olive paste into the sauce, then toss the pasta with the sauce and tip it into a warm serving bowl. Serve with freshly grated cheese.

Maccheroni con Salsa Messicana
Marlena's Mexican Fusion Pasta Bowl

Every so often I've gotta have my Mexican bowl of comfort: tender pasta tossed with lots of cheese and fiery chillies, studded with coriander leaves. It's wonderful on a late night or when you've just come in after a trying day. The green tomatillos, by the way, are utterly Mexican, and if you can't find any (usually in tins), they are easy to grow, even in grey, drizzly Britain. If not, add a squirt of lime juice.
SERVES 4

1 poblano or anaheim chilli, or large mild green chilli
1–2 small-to-medium green chillies, chopped, to taste
Several tablespoons chopped or sliced mild pickled green chillies (*jalapeños en escabeche*) or other pickled peppers, plus a little of the marinade
3–5 spring onions, thinly sliced
3 cloves garlic, finely chopped
½ bunch or several handfuls of fresh coriander, coarsely chopped
400g (14 oz) small elbow-shaped pasta
Salt
250g (9 oz) mature Cheddar cheese, coarsely grated
100g (4 oz) Parmesan or similar cheese, coarsely grated
About 4 tablespoons soured cream or crème fraîche
Drizzle of extra virgin olive oil
3–5 tablespoons Mexican green salsa or mashed green tomatillos, or the juice of ½ lime

Roast or grill the poblano or anaheim chilli until it is slightly charred all over. Seal it in a polythene bag or place it in a bowl and cover tightly with a lid. When it is cool enough to handle, peel off the skin. Removing the stalk and seeds, cut the pepper into strips and in a bowl combine with the fresh green chilli, the pickled chillies or peppers, the spring onions, garlic and coriander. Set aside.

Cook the pasta in a large pan of rapidly boiling salted water until *al dente*, then drain, return to the pan over a gentle heat and toss with the cheeses and soured cream. Scoop in the reserved chilli mixture and continue to toss, drizzling the olive oil over along with the salsa or lime juice.

Serve right away, melty, cheesey and spicy in bowls. I eat this with a spoon.

Pasta from the Dairy

Butter, cream and all things dairy are just made to be eaten with pasta, almost any sort of pasta. Ravishingly rich, pasta with cream is a special occasion dish for my daughter and me, one we gravitate towards guiltily, greedily, happily. Pasta with cream and almost anything else – porcini, a grating of truffle, a sprinkling of Gorgonzola, shreds of prosciutto and a few peas. And if none of these embellishments are around, just cream and lots of nutty freshly grated Parmesan; in fact, butter, cream and Parmesan give you the classic Fettuccine Alfredo – the only other ingredient you might consider is freshly grated nutmeg.

Of course, there is also billowy milky ricotta and its sidekick the creamy mascarpone, rich and complex fontina, pungent sheep's milk pecorino, all so delicious with the supple strands and shapes of pasta.
Each region of Italy has its own cheeses that are special to their own pastas. If you know a regional cheese that I haven't mentioned, there will always be pasta dishes that will accept it gracefully and deliciously.

Farfalle con Ricotta

Farfalle with Ricotta and Spring Onions

*Buttered pasta, tossed with ricotta and Parmesan and a sprinkling of spring onions,
is utter comfort food and terribly moreish. When I first ate it I laughed out loud
with delight: this very Italian dish was virtually the same thing I had grown up
eating, but being Eastern European Jews we called it* Lokshen mit Käse *(noodles
with cheese). It's creamy and rich but bland without the spring onions.*
SERVES 4–6

400g (14 oz) farfalle (butterflies), twists or orecchiette (ear-shaped pasta
   discs)
30–40g (1–1½ oz) butter
Salt and freshly ground black pepper
200g (7 oz) ricotta cheese
Freshly grated Parmesan or pecorino cheese, to taste
3–4 spring onions, thinly sliced

Cook the pasta in a large pan of rapidly boiling salted water until *al dente*. Drain
lightly then toss the hot pasta first with the butter and salt and pepper to taste, then
with the ricotta and finally with the Parmesan or pecorino and spring onions. Serve
while it's good and hot.

Pasta alla 'Nigel'

Nigel's Green Pasta with Goat's Cheddar and Fresh Basil Oil

Our great friend Nigel Patrick has adapted this recipe from a traditional Italian one. The little slab of pungent goat's cheese rests on top of the garlicky and basil-dressed pasta to be nibbled while you eat the dish. You could grate it into the pasta, but I prefer it this way. If goat's Cheddar is not available, use any pungent, slightly crumbly cheese.

SERVES 4–6

5–8 cloves garlic, finely chopped
6 tablespoons finely shredded fresh basil
5–6 tablespoons extra virgin olive oil
500g (1 lb 2 oz) fettuccine or tagliatelle verdi (flat, long green ribbons)
Freshly grated Parmesan cheese, to taste
150–200g (5–7 oz) goat's Cheddar cheese, or as desired, cut into 4 or 8
    slabs

Combine the garlic and basil with the oil and set aside to macerate while you prepare the pasta. Bring a large pan of salted water to a rapid boil and cook the pasta until *al dente*, then drain.

Toss the hot pasta with the garlic and basil oil, then serve it up in a big warmed bowl or on individual plates or bowls, each portion sprinkled with a bit of Parmesan and a slab or two of goat's Cheddar.

Tagliarini al Rosmarino in Nidi di Parmigiano

Tagliarini with Rosemary Cream in a Crisp Parmesan Bowl

Admittedly these nifty, crisply baked Parmesan-cheese bowls are rather gimmicky, but they are appealing – a wildish-looking 'bowl' of golden-brown tuiles of Parmesan, spilling out a tangle of pasta. In a village outside Alba, I ate this blanketed with fresh white truffles. At home, I tend to drizzle a bit of truffle oil over the pasta, which is very nice too.

The Parmesan bowls aren't as difficult to make as they sound but if you don't have the wherewithal, leave them flat to become crisp and break them up for garnish instead.

SERVES 6

300g (11 oz) fontina or mature Cheddar, or youngish pecorino or
    pecorino romano cheese, freshly grated
300g (11 oz) Parmesan, asiago or pecorino cheese, freshly grated
3 shallots, finely chopped
2 cloves garlic, finely chopped
40–60g (1½–2½ oz) unsalted butter
Several sprigs of fresh sage
Several sprigs of fresh rosemary
1 tablespoon brandy or grappa
125ml (4½ fl oz) dry white wine
250ml (9 fl oz) chicken or vegetable stock
250ml (9 fl oz) single cream
1 egg yolk, lightly beaten
450g (1 lb) fresh tagliarini (thin flat long ribbons), or similar
Truffle oil for drizzling (optional)

Preheat the grill to high.

To make the Parmesan bowls, combine all the fontina or pecorino cheese with two-thirds of the Parmesan or Parmesan-type cheese and divide into 6 portions. Making one at a time, arrange a portion of the cheese in the shape of a pancake 20–25cm (8–10 in) in diameter on a non-stick baking sheet. Place under the grill for about 7 minutes, turning the sheet if necessary for even heating and browning, until the cheese has melted, is golden-brown and crisp around the edges and a slightly lighter colour in the middle. Remove and allow it to cool for a moment or two, but not long enough for it to harden. Quickly loosen first the edges of the pancake, then the entire pancake from the sheet and invert it over an upturned bowl or cup, gently moulding the sides to form a bowl shape that flares out slightly at the edges. Leave the Parmesan bowl to become crisp on its mould and repeat until you have 6 bowls. Set them aside.

In a large pan, lightly sauté the shallots and half the garlic in 15g (½ oz) of the butter until softened, then add the sage, rosemary and brandy or grappa and cook for a moment or two before pouring in the wine. Simmer over a high heat until the liquid has evaporated to a few tablespoons, then pour in the stock and reduce it to about 125ml (4½ fl oz). Strain the liquid into another saucepan, pour in the cream and simmer over a high heat for about 5 minutes.

Place the egg yolk in a bowl, take a tablespoon or two of the hot cream sauce and quickly stir it into the egg yolk, repeat, then carefully stir the yolk mixture into the cream sauce in the pan. Continue stirring over a low heat until the sauce has thickened. Set aside and keep warm.

In a large pan of rapidly boiling salted water, cook the pasta until *al dente*, then drain and toss with the sauce, the remaining garlic, butter and grated cheese. Drizzle with the truffle oil, if using.

Serve the pasta nestled into and spilling out of the Parmesan bowls and eat right away.

Pasta dei Pastori

Pasta with Ricotta, Goat's Cheese and Rocket

The combination of snowy ricotta and tangy goat's cheese (or feta) is as close as you can get to the delicious and delicately flavoured fresh goat's ricotta eaten in Puglia and other remote parts of the Italian countryside. Use a soft, creamy goat's cheese. Strands of peppery rocket leaves and a handful of oily, salty black olives add a pungent contrast. Serve with a salad of juicy tomatoes and basil.

SERVES 4–6

400g (14 oz) pasta such as penne (quills), conchiglie (shells), or similar
Salt
200g (7 oz) ricotta, crumbled or mashed
3 cloves garlic, finely chopped
150g (5 oz) goat's cheese (or feta), crumbled
Large pinch of dried Italian oregano or mixed Italian herbs, including
    thyme
3–4 tablespoons extra virgin olive oil
20 oil-cured black olives, pitted and cut into quarters or small pieces
Several handfuls of wild rocket, cut into bite-sized pieces

Bring a large pan of salted water to the boil, cook the pasta until it is *al dente*, then drain lightly, reserving a little of the cooking water.

Meanwhile, mix together the ricotta, garlic, goat's cheese, herbs and olive oil.

When the pasta is ready, toss it with the cheese mixture and olives, then stir in the rocket and any of the reserved cooking liquid, if needed, and serve.

Pasta Caprina

Pasta with Sun-Dried Tomato and Goat's Cheese Pesto

Either penne or fettuccine are good pasta shapes for this rich and tangy goat's cheese mixture. The dish has no roots of authenticity; it is something I whipped up one day in a Tuscan holiday villa, using wonderful local ingredients.

The goat's-cheese mixture is also delicious as a filling for ravioli – bind it together with an egg and a little Parmesan to give it body, then spoon it on to the fresh pasta sheets and seal.

SERVES 4–6

3 cloves garlic, finely chopped
15–20 sun-dried tomatoes, either marinated ones, drained, or dried ones,
    soaked (*see page 23*)
150–200g (5–7 oz) light, creamy goat's cheese
Large pinch of fresh thyme leaves
3–4 tablespoons extra virgin olive oil, or as desired
Salt and freshly ground black pepper
350g (12 oz) penne (quills) or fettuccine (long flat ribbons)
15–20 fresh basil leaves, torn, thinly sliced, or coarsely chopped

In a food processor or blender or with a mortar and pestle, combine or crush the garlic with the sun-dried tomatoes, goat's cheese and thyme. Work in a tablespoon or two of olive oil and salt and pepper to taste.

Cook the pasta in a large pan of rapidly boiling salted water until *al dente*, then drain, reserving a spoonful or two of the hot cooking liquid. Toss the pasta with the remaining olive oil followed by the reserved hot cooking liquid, then toss in the cheese mixture and stir until it forms a creamy sauce. Serve with the fresh basil tossed in or sprinkled over.

Orecchiette alla Contadina

Little Pasta Ears with Spicy Tomato Sauce, Peas and Cheese

A little crumbled goat's, sheep's or feta cheese adds a piquancy to the little ear-shaped orecchiette and their spicy tomato and pea sauce. Instead of peas you could add broccoli, green beans, spinach, chard, or a handful of rocket leaves at the end.
SERVES 4

6 cloves garlic, thinly sliced
1–2 small dried chillies, crumbled
4–5 tablespoons extra virgin olive oil
150ml (5 fl oz) dry white wine
300g (11 oz) fresh or canned chopped tomatoes
4 tablespoons passata
Large pinch of dried oregano leaves, crumbled in the hands
125g (4½ oz) shelled fresh or frozen peas
3–4 tablespoons tomato purée
350g (12 oz) orecchiette (ear-shaped pasta discs)
Salt and freshly ground black pepper
150g (5 oz) feta cheese, preferably a creamy mild one, crumbled
4 tablespoons freshly grated Parmesan or pecorino cheese

In a large frying pan heat the garlic and chilli in the olive oil until lightly golden, then pour in the wine and simmer over a medium–high heat until reduced by about half. Add the tomatoes with the passata and continue to cook over a high heat for a few more minutes or until the mixture is thick and saucy. Stir in the oregano, peas and tomato purée and cook for a few minutes more until the peas are tender; frozen peas only need to be heated through.

Bring a large pan of salted water to the boil and cook the orecchiette until *al dente*. Drain, reserving a few spoonfuls of the cooking liquid, and toss the pasta and liquid with the sauce. Season to taste then toss with the feta and Parmesan cheese. Serve immediately.

Tagliatelle allo Zafferano
Tagliatelle in Saffron Cream with Prosciutto

This creamy, delicate saffron-flavoured dish, studded with shreds of salty prosciutto, is as close to the ultimate as it can get. Sometimes I have to eat it with my eyes closed, it's that good – I purr as I fork it up. And it is so easy to prepare.

Be sure to use good saffron with a brilliant hue and strong flavour, unadulterated by marigold or other flower petals. Usually, this is the most expensive saffron.

SERVES 4–6

Several pinches of saffron threads
250ml (9 fl oz) dry white wine
350ml (12 fl oz) single or whipping cream
Salt and freshly ground black pepper
400g (14 oz) egg tagliatelle (thin, long flat ribbons)
100–125g (4–4½ oz) prosciutto, cut or torn into strips
6–8 heaped tablespoons freshly grated Parmesan cheese
30–40g (1–1½ oz) butter, at room temperature

Heat a heavy, ungreased frying pan and lightly toast the saffron, then pour in the wine and simmer until it has reduced to about 2–3 tablespoons. Add the cream, keeping aside several tablespoons to stir in at the end. Cook the sauce until it foams up and boils, then simmer to a bright-yellow mixture, reducing by about a third or half. Season and set aside.

Meanwhile, cook the pasta in a large pan of rapidly boiling salted water until *al dente*. Drain, reserving several tablespoons of the cooking liquid to toss into the pasta with the cream sauce. (Cream gets very thick as it combines with pasta, and adding the cooking liquid helps to lighten the sauce.)

Stir the prosciutto into the sauce and gently heat through, then toss in the pasta, adding the reserved cooking liquid, and mix well. Stir in most of the Parmesan along with the butter and remaining spoonfuls of cream. Serve right away with the remaining Parmesan on top.

Pappardelle con Verdure Grigliate e Ricotta

Pappardelle with Pan-roasted Vegetables and Ricotta

Roasted vegetables make the sauce for this lusty pasta, while crisp breadcrumbs absorb the extra juices. Freshly grated Parmesan and dollops of snowy ricotta or light fresh goat's cheese complete the dish – I prefer to mix the two, as ricotta cheese is rich and bland while tangy goat's cheese gives it a more interesting flavour.

Any wide, flat pasta goes well with this sauce – even lasagne sheets.

SERVES 4–6

100g (4 oz) stale country bread, such as ciabatta
4–6 tablespoons extra virgin olive oil
8–10 ripe small-to-medium tomatoes, halved or quartered
½ red pepper, seeded and thinly sliced
1 small courgette, cut into thin flat strips
½ red onion, coarsely chopped
Salt and freshly ground black pepper
Pinch of sugar if needed
5–8 cloves garlic, finely chopped
2–3 tablespoons tomato purée
2 tablespoons pine nuts, raw or toasted
Handful of basil, roughly torn
350g (12 oz) pappardelle (long flat ribbons), or similar
150g (5 oz) ricotta or light fresh goat's cheese, or a mixture of the two
Freshly grated Parmesan, to taste

Make the breadcrumbs either by grating the bread over the holes of a large grater or in a food processor.

In a large, heavy frying pan heat 1 tablespoon of the olive oil and stir in the breadcrumbs, cooking over a medium–low heat until they sizzle and brown, turning every so often. Transfer them to a plate and set aside.

Heat the remaining oil in the pan and cook the tomatoes, pepper, courgette and onion over a medium heat until they are browned on one side. Before they burn, turn them over and continue to pan-roast them on the other side. Don't move them about too much as they will become mushy.

Season the vegetables with salt, pepper and a tiny pinch of sugar and gently stir in the garlic and tomato purée. Sprinkle on the pine nuts and basil, then cover the pan and turn off the heat, but keep warm.

Meanwhile, cook the pasta in a large pan of rapidly boiling salted water until *al dente*. Drain, reserving a spoonful or two of the cooking water.

Toss the hot pasta with the vegetables, along with the cooking water if dry. Tip on to a platter, sprinkle with the breadcrumbs and top with dollops of ricotta and a final flourish of Parmesan.

Pappardelle con Burro al Rosmarino

Pappardelle with Rosemary Butter

I ate this dish with roast chicken, the buttered pasta enriched with the juices from the pan. Delicious! Any roasted bird – chicken, duck, goose, quail – goes well with this pasta, as long as the pan juices are skimmed of fat, so you can enjoy the herb-infused butter. I'm throwing in a few meaty Italian sausages next time, too.

Of course, the rosemary-buttered noodles are also terrific on their own, with no more than a very generous grating of Parmesan.

SERVES 4–6

125g (4½ oz) unsalted butter
6 tablespoons finely chopped fresh rosemary
3–4 tablespoons snipped chives (optional)
400g (14 oz) fresh or dried egg pappardelle (long flat ribbons)
Salt and freshly ground black pepper
Generous amount of freshly grated Parmesan

Gently heat the butter together with the rosemary in a heavy saucepan until it has melted and is flavoured with the rosemary. Add the chives, if using, and set aside while you cook the pasta. The rosemary butter can be made up to a week ahead of time and kept in the fridge.

Bring a large pan of salted water to the boil and cook the pappardelle according to the packet instructions or, if fresh, for about 4 minutes, until *al dente*. Be careful not to let it overcook. Drain, reserving a small spoonful of the cooking water.

Toss the hot pasta with the rosemary butter and the reserved hot water. Season to taste and serve up in hot bowls blanketed with lashings of freshly grated Parmesan.

Pasta with Seafood

Just a handful of sweet briny prawns, a pair of little squid or some morsels of succulent lobster may not be enough for a meal on their own, but added to pasta can provide a satisfying dish of deliciousness.

In the coastal regions it is fish and seafood that flavours pasta rather than the heavy meat sauces beloved in the mountain regions.

Whole crab, simmered in a sauce of tomatoes and wine; handfuls of crawfish or langoustine; chunks of sweet lobster; a clattering of clams in their shells – all these delicacies of the sea make their way into the pasta of nearly every sea region of Italy's long, long coastline.

One caveat – pastas with fish do not usually have grated cheese added to them. The cheese flavour can overwhelm the delicacy of fish.

Spaghetti alle Vongole
Spaghetti with Clams, Neapolitan-style

Originally created in Naples, where the seafood is impeccably fresh, the tomatoes exploding with flavour, the cooks bursting with enthusiasm, this dish is an Italian classic. The first time I tasted it, I was a teenager in Naples: we were at a table set out on the cobblestones, and I still remember the intense flavour of the tomatoey pasta and the sweet nuggets of clam meat as I sucked them out of their shells.

To remove any sand from the clams, soak them in lightly salted water for 2 hours, changing the water from time to time, then rinse.

SERVES 4–6

5–6 cloves garlic, crushed
1 small dried peperoncino, or a pinch of crumbled dried chilli
6–8 tablespoons extra virgin olive oil
700g (1½ lb) tiny clams in shells, well scrubbed
150ml (5 fl oz) dry white wine
150g (5 oz) cherry tomatoes, halved
150g (5 oz) passata or chopped canned tomatoes
Salt and freshly ground black pepper
Tiny pinch of sugar, if needed
400g (14 oz) spaghetti, vermicelli or bucatini (long strands)
2 tablespoons freshly chopped parsley

Gently heat the garlic, chilli and olive oil in a large, heavy frying pan for a few moments, until sizzling but not brown, then add the clams. Turn the heat up high and shake the pan several times to coat the clams in the garlicky oil. Pour in the white wine and continue cooking over a high heat until the wine has been reduced by about half and the clams are starting to open, then add the cherry tomatoes and passata. Continue to cook until all the clams are open, discarding any that have not opened after 10 minutes. Season with salt if needed (clams are naturally salty), pepper and a pinch of sugar if the tomatoes are too acidic.

Meanwhile, cook the pasta in a large pan of rapidly boiling salted water until *al dente*, then drain and toss with the sauce.

Serve right away, hot and fragrant, sprinkled with parsley.

Spaghetti ai Frutti di Mare

Spaghetti with Mixed Seafood and Spicy Tomato Sauce

We were in Puglia for one of Susannah Gelmetti's Cookery Weeks in Italy. Chef Marco tossed hot pepper, olive oil and seafood into a pan and shook it with a vengeance, turning everything into a sauce in a matter of minutes. I have used much more garlic than Marco in this recipe as Italians do not always use a lot of it, even in dishes that to me cry out for it.

*I think this would be a marvellous dish to serve with black pasta, made with the ink from squid (*pasta nera*).*

SERVES 4–6

150ml (5 fl oz) extra virgin olive oil
4–5 cloves garlic, crushed
1–2 small dried chilli peppers, left whole
200g (7 oz) mussels in their shells, cleaned
200g (7 oz) clams in their shells, cleaned
100g (4 oz) fresh prawns
100g (4 oz) squid, cleaned and sliced
100g (4 oz) shelled scallops, sliced
100ml (4 fl oz) dry white wine
150g (5 oz) cherry tomatoes, halved
150g (5 oz) fresh or canned tomatoes, crushed, or passata
Salt and freshly ground black pepper
Several big handfuls of torn basil leaves
400g (14 oz) spaghetti
1–2 tablespoons freshly chopped parsley

Bring a large pan of salted water to the boil for the pasta.

Meanwhile, heat the olive oil with the garlic and chilli pepper in a large frying pan, until the garlic is just fragrant, then add the mussels and clams and cook, shaking, covered, for about 10 minutes or until they just start to open. Transfer to a bowl, discarding any that remain closed, and add the prawns, calamari and scallops to the pan. Cook only for a moment or two, until they just start to go opaque, then set aside with the mussels and clams. Discard the chilli.

Next pour the wine into the pan, and cook over a high heat until it has reduced to only a few spoonfuls, then add the cherry tomatoes and crushed tomatoes or passata. Season to taste and stir in the basil leaves. Simmer over a medium–high heat for 5–10 minutes.

Cook the pasta in the rapidly boiling water until *al dente*, then drain, reserving a few spoonfuls of cooking water.

Toss the pasta with the sauce, stir in the reserved seafood and cook over a medium–high heat for just 30 seconds or so, adding the reserved cooking water if necessary.

Serve right away, sprinkled with a little chopped parsley.

VARIATION

Omit the tomatoes and, instead, add a little stock of choice. Serve with chunky cavatelli (little hollowed-out oval pasta shapes) rather than spaghetti.

Pasta con Gamberi

Pasta with Spicy Sardinian Prawn Sauce

The brandy adds a wonderful scent and flavour to this dish but the alcohol must be burnt off first by flambéeing it, which could be dangerous if you don't follow the instructions carefully. If you burn too much of the brandy at once it can burst into high and fierce flames. To avoid this, I recommend burning it off gradually, in small amounts at a time

SERVES 4

4 tablespoons extra virgin olive oil
5–6 cloves garlic, coarsely chopped
1 dried chilli pepper, crumbled, or peperoncino, finely chopped
450g (1 lb) raw prawns, either shelled and cut into bite-sized pieces or left
    complete in their shells
125ml (4½ fl oz) brandy
400g (14 oz) canned chopped tomatoes
2 tablespoons (3–4 sprigs) very thinly sliced fresh basil
1–2 tablespoons freshly chopped parsley, preferably Italian flat-leaf
Salt to taste
Tiny pinch of sugar to taste
1 tablespoon tomato purée (optional – depends on the flavour of the
    canned tomatoes, and the thickness of the sauce)
350g (12 oz) bucatini (long tubular strands) or a chunky pasta

In a large, heavy frying pan combine the olive oil, garlic and chilli and cook over a medium heat until the garlic turns golden. Add the prawns and cook until the colour just begins to turn from translucent to opaque pink, which will only take a minute or two. Turn off the heat and remove the prawns to a plate, leaving behind as much of the oil, garlic and chilli as you can.

Pour a fifth of the brandy into a large metal ladle and, keeping it at arm's length, gently heat it over the flame of the hob or over a match held beneath it – ideally, you should have someone to help you. When the brandy has become very hot, ignite it with a long match, away from your face and clothes, and let it burn, then pour it into the pan (off the heat) in which you have sautéed the prawns. When the flames have died down, repeat the procedure with another fifth of the brandy, and keep repeating it until you have used it all up. It really is a lot of brandy, so do not try to do it all at once.

Return the pan to the heat to burn off any residual alcohol, still keeping your hair, face, sleeves, curtains etc., away from the pan just in case it whooshes up in flames again.

When all is calm, turn up the heat and stir in the tomatoes, basil, parsley, salt and pinch of sugar, if the tomatoes need it. Simmer, stirring, for about 5 minutes to incorporate the flavoursome oil into the tomatoes, then, if the sauce needs to be a bit richer, add the tomato purée and taste for seasoning. Return the prawns to the pan, turn down the heat and keep warm.

Meanwhile, cook the pasta in a large pan of rapidly boiling salted water until *al dente* and drain, reserving a few spoonfuls of the cooking water. Combine the pasta with the sauce and prawns, adding the reserved cooking water as needed. Then tip it all on to a serving platter and serve right away.

VARIATION:

In place of prawns, langoustines, lobster or lobster tails are brilliant. So too are tiger prawns – though sometimes what they gain in size they lose in flavour.

Fettuccine con Granchi e Piselli

Fettuccine with Creamy Crab and Peas

Delicate strands of pasta caught up in a creamy sauce of crab and peas, this dish is also good made with angel-hair pasta, or with the hearty buckwheat pasta, pizzoccheri. In a cross-cultural fusion state of mind, Japanese soba noodles go well in this recipe, too.

And although cheese with fishy pastas is usually frowned upon, Parmesan enhances this one beautifully.

SERVES 4–6

50g (2oz) unsalted butter
2 cloves garlic, chopped
250–450g (9 oz–1 lb) white crab meat
175g–200g (6–7 oz) shelled fresh or frozen petits pois
300–350ml (11–12 fl oz) single cream
350g (12 oz) fettuccine (flat long ribbons)
Dash of fresh lemon juice
50g (2 oz) or more Parmesan cheese, freshly grated
Salt and freshly ground black pepper

Melt the butter with the garlic over a gentle heat in a heavy frying pan, taking care not to fry the garlic, just let it flavour the butter. Stir in the crab meat to warm through, then add the peas and cream and heat until bubbles form around the edge of the pan.

Meanwhile, cook the pasta in a large pan of rapidly boiling salted water until just *al dente*. Drain, reserving a small spoonful or two of the cooking water.

Toss the hot drained pasta with the crab mixture, lemon juice, the reserved cooking water and about two-thirds of the Parmesan. Season to taste and serve immediately, sprinkled with the remaining cheese.

VARIATION

Another beautiful creamy crab sauce uses artichoke slices instead of peas. Trim down 2 or 3 medium-sized artichokes to their hearts, remove the chokes, slice them and brown in a little butter. Magic!

Spaghetti con Aragosta o Gamberi

Spaghetti with Langoustines, Crawfish or Prawns

Like so many towns throughout Italy, the old quarter of Cervo on the Ligurian Riviera spills down from the top of a hill to the sea. Winding cobbled streets centre on the main piazza and church, and at night it is enchanting to eat there on a terrace overlooking the sea.

Pasta with langoustines is a favourite here: the spaghetti is tossed with the briny shellfish and just enough of the light but savoury sauce to make it interesting.

Important: flambé the brandy with care…

SERVES 4–6

12 small raw langoustines, crawfish, or 16 large prawns in their shells
6 tablespoons extra virgin olive oil, plus extra if needed
5 cloves garlic, coarsely chopped or sliced
3 tablespoons brandy
125ml (4½ fl oz) dry white wine
125ml (4½ fl oz) fish or chicken stock
2 tablespoons tomato purée
Tiny pinch of crumbled dried chilli
Salt and freshly ground black pepper
Generous pinch of fresh crushed oregano leaves, or to taste
400g (14 oz) spaghetti

In a large pan sauté the shellfish in about 3 tablespoons of the olive oil until they just turn pink, then remove to a plate and keep warm. Add the rest of the oil to the pan and cook the garlic until lightly golden and fragrant. Remove and turn off the heat.

It's important that you flambé the brandy to burn off the alcohol 1 tablespoon at a time, because if you do it all at once the resulting whoosh of flames could cause injury and damage. Place a tablespoon of the brandy in a large metal ladle or spoon and, keeping your face and clothing well away, warm it from underneath with a lighted match; ideally, you should have someone to help you. When the brandy has become very hot, ignite it with a long match, away from your face and clothes, and let it burn. When the flame dies out, pour the liquid into the pan (off the heat) and repeat with the next tablespoonful of brandy, until it has all been used.

Add the wine, stock, tomato purée and chilli to the brandy and return the pan to a high heat. Simmer until the liquid has been reduced to a savoury and intense sauce.

Lower the heat, season with salt, pepper and oregano, add the reserved shellfish with any juices and keep warm.

Cook the pasta in a large pan of rapidly boiling salted water until just *al dente*, then drain, reserving a few tablespoons of the cooking water.

Push the shellfish over to the side of the pan, or return to the plate for a moment, while you toss the hot pasta with the sauce and reserved cooking water. Tip on to a platter and serve immediately with the shellfish on top.

VARIATION

Pasta con Cappe Sante
Scallops with Black Squid-ink Pasta

Really gorgeous, black squid-ink spaghetti, awash in a tomato-tinged sauce, garnished with white scallops and a sprinkling of green parsley. Use spaghetti or vermicelli that is black due to having been made with the ink from the squid – it doesn't add much in the way of flavour but it is so striking that it creates a delightful dish.

Prepare the pasta dish as above, substituting the langoustine, crawfish or prawns with 12–16 scallops, griddled until they are only slightly opaque and lightly browned. Remove the scallops to a plate while you make the sauce and, when they are cool enough to handle, slice each one into several pieces.

Cook the squid-ink spaghetti or vermicelli in place of the plain spaghetti, mix with the sauce and serve garnished with the scallops and sprinkled with freshly chopped parsley.

Fettuccine con Aragosta e Fave

Fettuccine with Lobster and Broad Beans

Garlicky butter, tender, peeled broad beans and chunks of briny lobster – what could be more succulent to toss with tender pasta?

SERVES 4–6

1 kg (2¼ lb) broad beans in their pods
Salt
125ml (4½ fl oz) extra virgin olive oil
40–50g (1½ –2 oz) butter
5–7 cloves garlic, finely chopped
2 tablespoons freshly chopped parsley
2 lobster tails
400g (14 oz) fettuccine (flat long ribbons) or vermicelli (little worms)
5 tablespoons fish stock
1 lemon, cut into wedges

Pod the broad beans and cook them in a small saucepan of boiling salted water until they are just tender. Drain and leave until they are cool enough to handle, then pop the tender beans out of their skins. Although time consuming, it's important to do this because the skin is tough.

Preheat the grill to high. Meanwhile heat together the olive oil, butter and garlic in a pan until the garlic is fragrant but not browned. Remove from the heat and add the parsley.

Brush a small amount of this garlic butter over the lobster tails and grill under a high heat. When they are cool enough to handle, cut the meat out of the shells, chop it into chunks and add to the butter mixture, along with the broad beans.

Cook the pasta in a large pan of rapidly boiling salted water until *al dente*, then drain and toss with the buttery sauce, lobster and broad beans over a gentle heat, moistening with the fish stock as needed. Serve garnished with lemon wedges.

Ziti con Pesce Spada e Menta
Ziti with Swordfish and Mint

This Sicilian peasant dish uses the foods that are so evocative of the island: swordfish, mint, tomatoes, pasta and olive oil. If you were to paint a portrait of Sicilian food, there are few more things you would add.
SERVES 4

2 cloves garlic, halved
3 tablespoons extra virgin olive oil, plus extra for drizzling
Handful of fresh mint leaves
300g (11 oz) swordfish steaks, cut into bite-sized pieces
3–4 ripe tomatoes, diced
125ml (4½ fl oz) dry white wine
1–2 tablespoons tomato purée
Salt and freshly ground black pepper
400g (14 oz) ziti or other tubular pasta
100g (4 oz) mozzarella cheese, diced

Heat the garlic in the olive oil with half the mint leaves in a large pan, until the garlic is golden. Add the swordfish and lightly brown all over. Remove the fish from the pan, add the tomatoes and sauté for a few minutes. Stir in the wine, boil for a few minutes, then add the tomato purée. Return the fish to the sauce and remove from the heat. Season to taste.

Cook the pasta in a large pan of rapidly boiling water until *al dente*, then drain, reserving a few spoonfuls of the cooking liquid. Toss the pasta with the fish and sauce, adding the cooking liquid to loosen the sauce. Scatter the cheese over the top, lightly tossing as you heap it into the serving bowl. Drizzle with extra oil and sprinkle with the rest of the mint, thinly sliced.

Bavette o Orecchiette con Gamberetti e Zucchine

Pasta with Prawns and Courgettes

This sauce not only goes well with the long strands of bavette but its full flavour is also maximised by the flat ear shapes of orecchiette. Black pasta, made with squid ink, and green spinach pasta are good choices too.

SERVES 4–6

3 cloves garlic, finely chopped
1 small dried chilli, crushed
150ml (5 fl oz) extra virgin olive oil
4–5 tender small courgettes with flowers, pistils removed, the flowers cut into strips
250g (9 oz) cherry tomatoes, halved
6 tablespoons dry white wine
250g (9 oz) raw prawns, shelled
Salt and freshly ground black pepper
400g (14 oz) bavette (flat long ribbons) or orecchiette (flat ear-shaped discs)
2 tablespoons freshly chopped parsley
Handful of rocket leaves, coarsely chopped

Heat the garlic and chilli for a few seconds in the olive oil in a large pan, until it smells warm and fragrant. Lightly sauté the courgette flowers, remove from the pan, shaking off any oil, and set aside. Add the tomatoes and courgettes and simmer over a medium–high heat for about 15 minutes, until the courgettes are just tender and the tomatoes slightly saucy.

Pour in the wine, turn up the heat and continue to cook for a minute or two, until the wine has evaporated by about half. Add the prawns and cook over a medium heat for just a few moments more, until they turn pink.

Meanwhile, bring a large pan of salted water to the boil and cook the pasta until *al dente*. Drain, reserving a few tablespoons of the cooking liquid for the sauce.

Toss the pasta with the sauce, adding a few spoonfuls of the cooking water, taste for seasoning, then turn it into shallow soup bowls and serve right away, garnished with the flowers, parsley and rocket leaves.

Pesce all' Isolana

Red Snapper with Peas and Saffron Pastina 'Pearls'

Small pearls of pasta give a delightful bite to a dish, creating a meal in a soup: round, slightly chewy little nubbins, with a texture something like pasta, something like couscous or – dare I say it – even tapioca. This Sardinian pasta is, like Israeli couscous, lightly toasted when made – both types can be used here. If you are making your own, grate the pasta dough over the large holes of a grater.
SERVES 4

3–5 cloves garlic, finely chopped
3 tablespoons extra virgin olive oil
Several pinches of saffron threads
Small pinch of crumbled dried chilli
2 ripe tomatoes, diced
250ml (9 fl oz) dry white wine
1 litre (1¾ pints) fish or chicken stock
2–3 tablespoons tomato purée
Salt and freshly ground black pepper
175g (6 oz) fresh shelled or frozen petit pois
250g (9 oz) small pasta, such as orzo or similar size (*see pages 11–12*)
Several pinches of dried oregano
4 small fillets red snapper, skin attached
1 lemon, cut into wedges
1 tablespoon freshly chopped parsley

Heat the garlic in a large pan with the olive oil, saffron and chilli, until the garlic begins to turn golden. Remove half of this mixture and reserve to brush on to the fish, then add the tomatoes and wine to the remaining oil in the pan. Cook over a high heat until the wine has nearly evaporated, then add the stock, tomato purée and salt and pepper to taste and bring it all to the boil. Add the peas, pasta and oregano and simmer over a medium heat, until the pasta is just *al dente*, then set aside.

Heat the grill to high and brush the fish with the reserved garlic and saffron oil. Grill on each side, until the skin is sizzling and crisp, and the flesh is barely cooked but is just turning opaque. If the fish are quite small you may only need to grill them on the skin side.

Divide the soup between serving bowls and top each with a fish fillet, drizzling any remaining oil on top. Serve with wedges of lemon and a sprinkling of parsley.

Tagliolini al Salmone Affumicato

Pasta with Mascarpone and Smoked Salmon

Pasta with mascarpone and smoked salmon has become quite the fashionable thing, yet is traditional in style. Sometimes it's flambéed with a little vodka or brandy instead of white wine; and sometimes cream is used instead of mascarpone. One thing is certain – it's rich, rich, rich. Salmon offcuts or trimmings are perfect for this recipe. And although fishy pastas are never usually served with Parmesan, this one can be. Or you could replace it with caviar, as in the photograph...
SERVES 4–6

4 tablespoons unsalted butter
½ red onion, finely chopped
125ml (4½ fl oz) dry white wine
250g (9 oz) mascarpone cheese
100g (4 oz) smoked salmon, cut into strips
Freshly ground black pepper
400g (14 oz) fresh tagliolini or other thin flat pasta such as fettuccine or
    tagliarini
2 or more tablespoons freshly grated Parmesan cheese
4–6 tablespoons freshly chopped chives

Melt the butter in a heavy frying pan and lightly sauté the red onion; when it has softened, pour in the wine and cook over a high heat, until only about 2–3 tablespoons remain. Remove from the heat. Stir in the mascarpone cheese, then the salmon. Season with black pepper (smoked salmon is salty so you may not need extra salt) and set it aside.

Cook the pasta in a large pan of rapidly boiling salted water until it is *al dente*; fresh pasta cooks very quickly – 2–3 minutes – so don't let your attention stray. Drain, reserving a small amount of the cooking liquid, then toss the pasta into the sauce mixture, adding a few spoonfuls of the cooking liquid as needed. Stir in the Parmesan, sprinkle over the chives and serve.

Linguine con Tonno e Limone
Linguine with Tuna and Lemon

As well as linguine, this is good with penne or any other chunky pasta. It's a quickly tossed together dish that is perfect for a midnight supper or cosy lunch, very la dolce vita, *and made with ingredients that most people have to hand in the store cupboard. A good way to use that little bit of wine left over from last week's dinner party.*
SERVES 4–6

2 tablespoons capers, or as desired
4–5 cloves garlic, coarsely chopped
4–6 tablespoons extra virgin olive oil
4–6 anchovies, finely chopped
2 x 180g (6 oz) cans tuna chunks, drained and broken up
175ml (6 fl oz) dry white wine
Grated zest and juice of 1 lemon
400g (14 oz) linguine (long flat strands)
2–3 tablespoons stale, toasted or dried plain breadcrumbs, or as needed
Freshly ground black pepper
1–2 tablespoons freshly chopped flat-leaf parsley

If using capers preserved in vinegar, rinse them in cold water, drain and set aside. If using salted capers, soak in cold water while you prepare the rest of the dish.

Lightly sauté the garlic in the olive oil in a large pan until it colours lightly, then add the anchovies and cook together until they just melt. Carefully stir in the tuna without breaking it up too much, then pour in the wine and cook over a high heat until it has evaporated by about half. Add the drained capers and the grated lemon zest and set the sauce aside.

Cook the pasta in a large pan of rapidly boiling salted water until *al dente*, then drain, reserving a few spoonfuls of the cooking liquid.

Toss the hot pasta with the sauce over the heat, adding a spoonful or two of the cooking liquid and stirring in the breadcrumbs, until it all comes together. Squeeze lemon over it, sprinkle with pepper, toss once more and serve right away, garnished with parsley.

Spaghetti con Calamari e Piselli

Spaghetti with Squid and Peas

So delicious, this stew of squid and peas. Serve with penne if you like instead of spaghetti – I think it would be very nice served with black penne, made with the ink of the squid. This sauce is also wonderful spooned over crisp crostini or bruschetta as an antipasto, or heaped on to a bread roll for a panino *to remember.*
SERVES 4–6

4–6 tablespoons extra virgin olive oil
4 cloves garlic, finely chopped
3 anchovies, finely chopped
Pinch of crumbled dried chilli, or to taste
400g (14 oz) squid, cleaned and cut into rings, the tentacles into bite-sized lengths
250ml (9 fl oz) dry white wine
2 tablespoons tomato purée
200g (7 oz) young tender blanched fresh (or frozen) petits pois
2 tablespoons freshly chopped parsley
Salt and freshly ground black pepper
400g (14 oz) spaghetti

Gently heat the olive oil in a large pan and lightly sauté the garlic and anchovies with the chilli for a moment or two. Stir in the squid and lightly cook it for a few minutes, then remove the squid from the pan and set aside.

Pour in the wine and cook over a high heat until it evaporates to about 100ml (4 fl oz), then stir in the tomato purée, peas, parsley and squid. Remove from the heat.

Cook the spaghetti in a large pan of rapidly boiling salted water until *al dente*, then drain and reserve some of the cooking water.

Reheat the sauce, then toss with the pasta, adding a little of the reserved cooking liquid. Season to taste and serve up.

Pasta con le Sarde

Pasta with Sardines

Sicily's favourite dish, Pasta con le Sarde, *is a symphony of flavours and textures. It's also a portrayal of the island's history: the sweet and sour of the Arab invaders, the lusty olivey scent of Greece and saffron from the East. Toasted breadcrumbs give the pasta a bit of bite (*la mollica*) in the way that pastas from the south often do, and the fish, the fresh sardines, taste of the Sicilian sea.*

SERVES 4–6

100g (4 oz) stale bread
7 tablespoons extra virgin olive oil
175–200g (6–7 oz) wild fennel, plus the feathery fronds, or ½ large bulb
    fennel or 1 whole small-to-medium bulb fennel, coarsely chopped
2 teaspoons fennel seeds
1 onion, chopped
3–5 cloves garlic, finely chopped
2–3 tablespoons raisins
2–3 sun-dried tomatoes, chopped or cut into small pieces
2 pinches saffron threads, soaked in 125ml (4½ fl oz) hot water
½ stock cube or a shake or two of liquid concentrated stock
Freshly ground black pepper
12–15 fresh sardines, filleted
7–8 anchovy fillets, rinsed and coarsely chopped
350g (12 oz) bucatini (long tubular strands) or penne (quills)
2 tablespoons pine nuts

Make breadcrumbs, either by grating the bread or by whizzing it in a food processor or blender, and lightly brown them in a tablespoon of the olive oil in a heavy frying pan. Keep tossing and turning them so they don't burn. Remove from the heat.

Bring a large pan of water to the boil and cook the fennel and fennel seeds for 15-20 minutes. Remove from the heat and drain, saving the water for cooking the pasta. If using wild fennel, it will be tough and need to be chopped some more, either in a food processor or with a chef's knife; if it is cultivated fennel, then this is not necessary.

In another pan, lightly sauté the onion and garlic in half the remaining olive oil and cook until softened but not browned. Add the cooked fennel, currants, sun-dried tomatoes, saffron water, stock cube, black pepper and about 250 ml (9 fl oz) of the fennel water and cook over a medium heat for about 10 minutes.

Lightly brown the sardines and anchovies in the remaining olive oil in a heavy frying pan over a medium–low heat. Break some of the sardines apart, mashing them a little with a fork, reserving a fillet or two per person for garnish. Scrape the contents of the pan into the fennel mixture.

Return the remaining fennel water to the heat and bring it to the boil and cook the pasta in it until just *al dente*. Drain lightly and toss with the sardine sauce, breadcrumbs and pine nuts, then divide between serving plates. Finish by arranging the reserved sardine fillets in the centre.

VARIATION

This is also delicious without fish, simply a bowl of pasta with the sweet, tart, crisp, herbal flavours of Sicily. Omit the sardines and anchovies and replace them with a handful of coarsely chopped black oil-cured olives.

Pasta with Meats and Poultry

All I have to do to achieve sensual heaven is think of prosciutto – a salty, sweet and silky ham – cut into strips and tossed with pasta. Whatever else is included is deliciously irrelevant: olive oil or butter, egg or cream, Parmesan or pecorino – it's the shreds of prosciutto that make such a dish sublime and give it a personality of its own. Bresaola, a similar meat made with beef, creates the same effect. Other meats, too, perk up a dish of pasta no end: pieces of pancetta, morsels of mortadella, bites of any of the many spicy salamis can all be added at your whim and desire.

Italy's regions abound with specialities – each has its own sausage and ham – and wild meats such as rabbit and duck proliferate deep in the countryside of Tuscany and Umbria and in the northern pasturelands of Piedmont. Chicken isn't a traditional ingredient in pasta sauces but is growing in popularity and nowadays is often found enriching a wholesome savoury sauce.

Spaghetti con Sugo D'Agnello
Spaghetti with Spicy Lamb Sauce

This little pasta dish from Abruzzo – the region where lamb is the meat of choice and shepherds roam the countryside – is as spicy as the amount and type of chilli or peperoncino you use. But please, have more sense than I had once: give it a good pinch or two of heat, but don't napalm your mouth. You can also make this with either rabbit or chicken breast, but omit the cheese.

SERVES 4–6

2 small-to-medium lamb chops, cutlets or noisettes (about 200g/7 oz in total), fat removed
3–5 tablespoons extra virgin olive oil
10–15 cloves garlic, thinly sliced
Several large pinches of crumbled dried chilli or peperoncino, as desired
250ml (9 fl oz) dry white wine
Salt and freshly ground black pepper
Several pinches of oregano leaves, preferably Italian
400g (14 oz) spaghetti
Freshly grated pecorino cheese, to taste

Cut the lamb into tiny slices, juliennes or shreds. Heat the olive oil in a large pan and brown the lamb with the garlic and chilli, taking care not to brown the garlic too much.

Pour in the wine and cook over a high heat until it has reduced by about half, then season to taste and sprinkle in the oregano. Remove from the heat while you cook the pasta.

In a large pan of rapidly boiling salted water, cook the spaghetti until just *al dente*, then drain, reserving a few spoonfuls of the cooking liquid. Toss the pasta over a medium heat with the sauce, adding the cooking liquid, and blend well.

Serve right away, tossed with a little freshly grated cheese if desired.

Rigatoni con Salsa di Coniglio, Spinaci e Porcini

Rigatoni with a Sauce of Rabbit, Spinach and Porcini

This Tuscan-inspired dish is also good made with minced chicken or turkey instead of rabbit. The woodsy flavours of the porcini and leafy spinach make a luscious sauce that gets trapped inside the tubular pasta.

SERVES 4–6

1 small packet dried porcini, about 15g (½ oz)
750g (1 lb 10 oz) boneless rabbit meat or unskinned chicken thighs, cut into small pieces
3 tablespoons extra virgin olive oil
1 onion, chopped
Salt and freshly ground black pepper
1 sprig fresh rosemary
Pinch of fennel seeds
3–4 cloves garlic, coarsely chopped
500g (1 lb 2 oz) fresh spinach leaves, washed and shredded
250ml (9 fl oz) dry white wine
3 medium-sized ripe tomatoes or 2 large tomatoes, diced
500g (1 lb 2 oz) rigatoni, penne rigate or other pasta tubes
Freshly grated Parmesan cheese, to taste

Place the porcini in a bowl and pour 350ml (12 fl oz) boiling water over them. Cover and leave to rehydrate for 30 minutes. Mince the meat in a food processor.

Heat a large frying pan until it is quite hot then add the olive oil, minced meat, onion and seasoning and fry for 5 minutes or so, turning the meat every so often, until it is browned in places and in chunks; do not cook it all the way through. Add the rosemary, fennel, garlic and spinach, then pour in the white wine. Cook over a high heat until the wine has almost disappeared.

Drain the porcini, reserving their soaking water, chop them and add to the meat mixture. Pour in the soaking water, taking care to leave behind any grit and sand. Cook over a high heat for 5–10 minutes or until the sauce has slightly reduced and intensified in flavour.

Add the tomatoes and cook for a few minutes more so that they blend into the sauce, then set aside while you cook the pasta.

In a large pan of rapidly boiling salted water cook the rigatoni until *al dente*, then drain, reserving a few tablespoons of the cooking water. Toss the pasta into the sauce, along with the cooking water and a few tablespoons of the Parmesan. Serve right away, with extra Parmesan as desired.

Pappardelle al Sugo Antico

Ribbons of Pasta with an Old-fashioned *Ragù* Sauce

This is a lusty Tuscan sauce, full of various meats and redolent of mushrooms and artichokes, all tomatoey and luscious. Flat, wide pasta such as pappardelle is great with this ragù. *And it's also delicious ladled over polenta.*

SERVES 6–8

20g (¾ oz) dried porcini
500ml (18 fl oz) dry white wine
100g (4 oz) pancetta, unsmoked bacon or prosciutto, chopped
1 onion, finely chopped
350g (12 oz) minced beef, pork or lamb
1 chicken breast or 2 thighs or 200g (7 oz) turkey, diced
400g (14 oz) ripe fresh or canned tomatoes, chopped
3 tablespoons tomato purée
Pinch of sugar, if needed
Dried oregano, to taste
2–3 artichoke hearts, cut into bite-sized pieces
Salt and freshly ground pepper
400g (14 oz) pappardelle (large, long flat ribbons)
Freshly grated Parmesan, asiago or pecorino cheese, to taste

Place the dried mushrooms in a pan with half the wine mixed with 250ml (9 fl oz) water, bring to the boil, then reduce the heat and simmer for 15–20 minutes. Lift out the mushrooms with a slotted spoon and squeeze them over the cooking liquid still in the pan. Chop them coarsely and set aside. Strain the mushroom liquor carefully into a bowl and also set aside.

In a large pan, sauté the pancetta and onion until the onion is translucent, then add the minced beef and chicken and brown over a medium heat. Add the mushrooms and their cooking liquid with the tomatoes, tomato purée, remaining white wine, sugar and oregano. Bring to the boil, then reduce the heat and simmer for 15–20 minutes or until the chicken is cooked. Add the artichokes, simmer for a few more minutes and taste for seasoning, stirring in more tomato purée if necessary.

Cook the pappardelle in a large pan of rapidly boiling salted water until *al dente* then drain, reserving a spoonful or two of the cooking water. Toss the hot pasta with the hot sauce, adding some of the cooking water to bring the dish together, then serve up with the cheese as desired.

Fettuccine alla Papalina

Fettuccine with Peas, Prosciutto and Raw Egg

Delicious with home-made or dried egg pasta, this Roman dish consists of tender strands of fettuccine flavoured with beaten egg and cheese, alla carbonara, then tossed with peas and prosciutto. The title translates as 'Pope's pasta' and was given to this dish in honour of Cardinal Pacelli when he became Pope Pius XII. It was his favourite recipe.

Mange-touts, cooked and cut into strips, are also delicious along with, or in place of, the peas, as are thinly sliced spring onions or asparagus. Sugar-snap peas would go very well, too.

SERVES 4

1 large or 2 small-to-medium onions, chopped
40–50g (1½ –2oz) unsalted butter
250g (9 oz) fresh blanched or frozen petits pois
125ml (4½ fl oz) chicken or vegetable stock
100g (4 oz) prosciutto, cut into strips
2 eggs, lightly beaten
125g (4½ oz) freshly grated Parmesan cheese
Salt and freshly ground black pepper
400g (14 oz) fettuccine (flat long ribbons) or 1 recipe home-made egg
      fettuccine (*see page 15*)
Extra Parmesan cheese for grating

Lightly sauté the onion in the butter in a large pan until soft and golden, then add the peas and stock. Turn up the heat and simmer for about 5 minutes until the peas are bright green and the sauce has been reduced by about a half. Remove from the heat and stir in the prosciutto.

Meanwhile mix the egg with the Parmesan in a bowl, season to taste and set aside.

In another large pan, cook the fettuccine in rapidly boiling salted water until just *al dente*, then drain, reserving about 100ml (4 fl oz) of the cooking water.

Toss the hot pasta with the egg mixture, coating each strand evenly, then tip it into the sauce in the pan. Mix together for a few moments over a gentle heat, adding the reserved cooking water a tablespoon at a time.

Serve right away, with extra Parmesan for grating.

Fettuccine Voluttuose

Fettuccine with a Voluptuous Sauce of Duck and Porcini

This recipe is so elegant, so succulent, so full of ducky flavour and rich with cream, that you might find it one of your all-time favourites as it is mine – especially for very special dinner parties. It has a secret ingredient, however – the carcass of a duck. If you're ever served roast duck at a party, ask your hosts if you can take the carcass home. I'm not above this – but then again, I don't get invited to a lot of parties!

SERVES 4

1 raw duck carcass, breasts and legs trimmed off
1 head garlic, broken into cloves and unpeeled
1 onion, cut into chunks
3 carrots, diced
2 bay leaves
Sprig or two of thyme
Sprig or two of rosemary
Salt and freshly ground black pepper
5 tablespoons brandy or grappa
500ml (18 fl oz) white or red wine
500ml (18 fl oz) chicken or beef stock
30g (1 oz) dried mushrooms such as porcini or a mixture of dried wild
    mushrooms, broken into small pieces
400g (14 oz) fresh or canned tomatoes, chopped
500ml (18 fl oz) single cream
500g (1 lb 2 oz) fettuccine (flat long ribbons)
1 tablespoon freshly chopped parsley
Freshly grated Parmesan cheese, to taste

Preheat the oven to 200–220°C/400–425°F/Gas 6–7.

Place the duck carcass in a flameproof roasting pan, unless it is already roasted, with the garlic, onion, carrot and bay leaves and roast for about 40 minutes or until the bones and vegetables are dark brown in spots. If you have any duck giblets, including the liver, add them to the pan about halfway through.

Remove from the oven and add the thyme and rosemary, salt and pepper, brandy, wine and stock. Bring to the boil over a high heat, stirring up all the residue stuck on the bottom. Pour it all into a large stockpot and bring back to the boil. Reduce the heat and leave to simmer, covered, for 1½ hours.

Remove from the heat, lift out the carcass and leave to cool. Strain the liquid, pressing the solids to extract as much flavour as possible, and pour into another large saucepan. Bring back to the boil, add the dried mushrooms and tomatoes and simmer uncovered for 30–40 minutes more, adding a little more wine, stock, or water as the liquid reduces. You want a concentrated sauce that's not burnt or bitter.

Pour in the cream and return to the boil. Cook over a medium–high heat for 15–20 minutes, until the liquid has reduced down to a very rich sauce.

When the carcass is cool enough to handle, peel off any meat and discard the bones. Add the shreds of duck meat to the sauce, season to taste and set aside.

Cook the fettuccine in a large pan of rapidly boiling salted water until *al dente*, then drain, reserving a spoonful or two of the cooking liquid. Toss the hot pasta with the sauce and a little of the cooking liquid as necessary. Serve sprinkled with parsley and Parmesan to taste and eat right away.

Pasta con Ragù alla Paesana

Pasta with Braised Chicken Thighs, Spicy Tomato Sauce, Meat and Spinach

A Sicilian dish to be eaten in two courses – the pasta with the sauce followed by the meat – in true rustic Italian style. This is my kind of pasta: it includes a whole head – testa d'aglio – of garlic.

A sauce like this one is not worth making for one or two people. For more than four to six mouths to feed, add several Italian sausages cut into bite-sized pieces. Left-over sauce freezes beautifully, and is delicious on nearly anything.

SERVES 4–6

3 tablespoons extra virgin olive oil
4–8 chicken thighs
500g (1 lb 2 oz) meat such as pork, lamb, beef, rabbit, in chunks
1 onion, chopped
1 carrot, chopped
1 stalk celery, chopped
1 green pepper or Italian frying pepper, diced
Pinch of fennel seeds
250ml (9 fl oz) dry red wine
600–800g (1 lb 5 oz–1¾ lb) fresh or canned tomatoes
1 head of garlic, cut in half horizontally
250ml (9 fl oz) stock
85ml (3 fl oz) brandy or grappa
3 bay leaves
Several large pinches of mixed dried Italian herbs
Sprig of fresh rosemary
Handful of dried mushrooms, broken into small pieces
5 or so juniper berries, or a tot of gin
500g (1 lb 2 oz) fresh spinach, washed, dried and shredded
500g (1 lb 2 oz) pappardelle (large, long flat ribbons) or other similar pasta
Freshly grated Parmesan or pecorino cheese, to taste

Heat half the olive oil in a large frying pan, brown the chicken and meat together or in turns, then remove to a casserole off the heat.

Add the remaining oil to the frying pan and sauté the onion with the carrot, celery, green pepper and fennel seeds, until the vegetables are soft, then tip them into the casserole.

Next pour the wine into the pan, turn up the heat and cook it for a minute or so, stirring all the time, so that the wine picks up all the flavours. Pour this on to the meat and vegetables in the casserole.

Add the tomatoes, garlic, stock, brandy or grappa, bay leaves, herbs, rosemary, mushrooms, juniper berries or gin to the casserole, heat it to boiling point, turn the heat down and leave to simmer, covered, for about an hour until the chicken and meats are tender and cooked. Add the spinach to the casserole and continue to cook, uncovered, for a few minutes more, until tender.

Cook the pasta in a large pan of rapidly boiling salted water until *al dente*. Drain, saving some of the cooking water. Toss the cooked pasta in a serving dish with some of the sauce from the casserole, a spoonful or two of the cooking water, and stir in some Parmesan. Serve with more sauce and Parmesan and enjoy the meat casserole to follow.

Pasta Mezzogiorno
Pasta with Meaty Tomato and Fennel Sauce

Ah, one of those lusty and robustly sauced pastas that make you feel a bit like Sophia Loren in a 1950s movie.

SERVES 4

1 onion, chopped
3 cloves garlic, finely chopped
50g–100g (2–4 oz) pancetta, diced
3–4 tablespoons extra virgin olive oil
125g (4½ oz) pork loin or shoulder, thinly sliced
½ bulb fennel, chopped
¼ teaspoon dried oregano leaves, or to taste
175ml (6 fl oz) dry red wine
250ml (9 fl oz) meat stock
400g (14 oz) fresh or canned tomatoes, chopped
¼–½ teaspoon fennel seeds
1–3 teaspoons finely chopped fresh rosemary, or to taste
3 heaped tablespoons tomato purée
Salt and freshly ground black pepper
Pinch of sugar, if needed
400g (14 oz) penne or similar
250g (9 oz) fresh ricotta cheese
50g (2 oz) Parmesan cheese, freshly grated

Lightly sauté the onion, garlic and pancetta in the olive oil in a large pan, until the onions are golden, then turn up the heat and stir in the meat so that it browns.

Add the fennel, cook for a few moments, then sprinkle with the oregano and pour in the red wine and stock. Continue to cook over a high heat until the liquid has reduced in volume by about a third or a half, and the flavours have intensified.

Add the tomatoes, fennel seeds and rosemary. Lower the heat and cook, covered, simmering slowly for 30–40 minutes, until the sauce is rich and flavourful and the meat is tender. If the sauce is too thin, remove the lid and leave it to evaporate.

Stir in the tomato purée, taste for seasoning and add a tiny pinch of sugar if the sauce seems too acidic. Keep warm while you cook the pasta.

Bring a large pan of salted water to the boil and cook the pasta until it is *al dente*, then drain and toss with the sauce. Serve right away, garnished with dollops of ricotta and freshly grated Parmesan.

Perciatelli con Cavolfiore e Salsicce

Fat Spaghetti with Spicy Cauliflower and Sausage Sauce

Perciatelle strands are chewy and toothsome, and with lashings of sauce are deliciously messy to eat. You can use any colour pepper, but I find orange peppers the perfect foil for the other colours and flavours of this dish.
SERVES 4–6

1 medium-sized orange pepper, seeded and diced
1 medium-sized or 2 medium–small onions, chopped
4 tablespoons extra virgin olive oil
1 small-to-medium cauliflower (about 750g/1 lb 10 oz), cut into small
    florets
5–8 cloves garlic, coarsely chopped
3 stalks celery, chopped
2–3 teaspoons fennel seeds
Pinch or two of crumbled dried chilli
1–2 meaty Italian sausages, cut into bite-sized pieces
800g (1¾ lb) canned tomatoes, chopped, including the juice
Pinch of sugar
Several sprigs of fresh thyme
Grated zest of ½ lemon
400g (14 oz) perciatelli (fat spaghetti) or similar
Salt and freshly ground black pepper
Freshly grated Parmesan cheese, to taste (optional)

In a large pan, lightly sauté the pepper and onion in the olive oil until they begin to soften, then add the cauliflower and half the garlic and continue to cook over a medium low heat for 5–10 minutes, or until the cauliflower starts to turn golden.

Add the celery, fennel, chilli and sausage and continue to brown together for a further 5–10 minutes. Then stir in the tomatoes, sugar, thyme, lemon zest and remaining garlic and leave to cook over a medium heat until the sauce thickens.

Cook the perciatelli in a large pan of rapidly boiling salted water until *al dente*, then drain, saving a spoonful or two of the cooking water. Toss the hot pasta with the sauce and the cooking water. Season to taste and sprinkle with Parmesan cheese if desired.

Spaghetti al Marsala
Spaghetti with Sausage, Olives and Marsala

The sweet-wine flavour of Sicilian Marsala combines deliciously with the chunky bites of spicy, herby sausage and salty olives with a dash of robust tomatoes which make up this sauce created in the shadow of Mount Etna. This is as easy to toss together as it is to eat.
SERVES 4–6

300g (11 oz) Italian sausage, preferably herby and a little spicy, cut into chunks
3 tablespoons extra virgin olive oil
5–8 cloves garlic, coarsely chopped
Pinch of crumbled dried chilli, or as desired
125ml (4½ fl oz) dry Marsala (or dry fino sherry mixed with a little port)
Large sprig of fresh rosemary
1 large or 2 small-to-medium ripe tomatoes, diced, or 2 tablespoons canned chopped tomatoes
25 mixed olives, green and black, stoned and sliced
400g (14 oz) spaghetti
Salt and freshly ground black pepper
Freshly grated Parmesan cheese, to taste

Brown the sausage in a heavy frying pan, then remove and set aside on a plate to keep warm. In the same pan add the olive oil, garlic and chilli, and cook gently for a few moments until the garlic is fragrant but not browned. Pour the Marsala into the pan and add the rosemary, then turn up the heat and simmer until the liquid has reduced by about half. Stir in the tomatoes and reserved sausage and cook together until the mixture is deliciously saucy, about 5–10 minutes. Don't let it burn – the sauce will be thin but intense and there won't be much of it. Remove from the heat and add the olives.

Cook the spaghetti in a large pan of rapidly boiling salted water until *al dente*, then drain, reserving a few tablespoons of the cooking liquid. Toss with the sauce, adding a spoonful or two of the cooking liquid to hold it all together, and check the seasoning (the olives are salty so you'll probably not need salt). Serve, with Parmesan sprinkled over.

Pasta Piccante Abruzzese con Prosciutto e Zucchine

Pasta Abruzzo-style with Prosciutto and Courgettes

This lusty vegetable and prosciutto sauce is from the Abruzzo, on the Adriatic coast in central Italy, said to be the home of the nation's best pasta. Why? The water, the wheat and the tools which create the miniscule ridges that hold the sauce like a magnet. For this dish, I prefer gigli, the lily-shaped, ruffle-edged pasta that wraps itself around the nuggets of sauce so well, but any other pasta with nooks and crannies in it, such as penne or conchiglie, will do.

SERVES 4

2 large red or yellow peppers
1 onion, finely chopped
1 small-to-medium courgette, diced
4 tablespoons extra virgin olive oil
100g (4 oz) prosciutto, cut into shreds
5–7 cloves garlic, chopped
425 (15 oz) canned chopped tomatoes or 600g (1 lb 5 oz) fresh tomatoes, chopped, with 2 tablespoons tomato purée
2 pinches of crumbled dried chilli
150ml (5 fl oz) dry white wine or stock
Pinch of mixed dried Italian herbs or oregano
Pinch of sugar
Salt and freshly ground black pepper
450g (1 lb) gigli (see above), penne (quills) or conchiglie (shells)
5 tablespoons freshly grated Parmesan or pecorino cheese, plus extra for serving if desired
10–15 leaves or more fresh basil, shredded
4 large tablespoons ricotta cheese

Preheat the grill to high and grill the peppers until they are charred and blackened all round – watch them carefully and keep turning them. Place in a bowl, cover and leave for at least 15 minutes or until they are cool enough to handle.

Meanwhile, lightly sauté the onion and courgette in the olive oil in a large pan until softened, then stir in the prosciutto and garlic. Keep stirring for a few moments and remove from the heat.

Peel and coarsely chop the peppers, discarding the skin, stem and seeds, and add them with their juices to the pan along with the tomatoes, chilli, wine, dried herbs and sugar. Season to taste. Return to the heat and bring to the boil, then reduce the heat and simmer to thicken the sauce while you cook the pasta.

Bring a large pan of salted water to the boil and cook the pasta until *al dente*; the length of time will depend on the type of pasta you use. Drain and toss with the sauce, Parmesan and basil, then serve in large bowls each topped with a dollop of ricotta and, if desired, a little extra basil and Parmesan.

Spaghetti alla Carbonara

Even the mayor of Rome dishes up steaming plates of Spaghetti alla Carbonara *to impress. This concoction of hot pasta tossed in raw egg and cheese and generously studded with pieces of pancetta or bacon is saucy, succulent and rich, rich, rich!*
SERVES 4–6

125g (4½ oz) pancetta, or unsmoked rindless bacon, diced
2 tablespoons extra virgin olive oil
1 onion, finely chopped
1 clove garlic, finely chopped
Salt and freshly ground black pepper
400g (14 oz) spaghetti
3–4 eggs, lightly beaten
125ml (4½ fl oz) cream or chicken stock
100g (4 oz) or more freshly grated Parmesan and/or pecorino romano
   cheese
1–2 tablespoons freshly chopped flat-leaf parsley

Lightly brown the pancetta in the olive oil in a large pan over a medium-low heat. Remove it from the pan with a slotted spoon and cook the onion and garlic in the oil until the onion is soft; do not let them brown. Season with pepper to taste.

Bring a large pan of water to the boil then add a tablespoon of salt. Cook the spaghetti in this, until just *al dente*, then drain, reserving about 125ml (4½ fl oz) of the cooking water.

Meanwhile combine the egg, cream or stock and cheese in a bowl. Then return the pancetta to the pan with the onions and garlic and warm through. Toss the hot pasta and the egg mixture into the pancetta and onions quickly, taking care to coat each strand of spaghetti. Add enough of the reserved cooking water to make the pasta creamy and succulently moist. It should be moistened more than you want it to be, as the pasta will keep absorbing the liquid as it travels from stove to table.

Serve it up with a hit of extra pepper and cheese, if desired, and a sprinkling of parsley.

Quick, Quick Pasta

Home at the end of a long day, you scan your store cupboard (*see pages 20–23*) to see what you can ferret from the shelves. The Italians have a word for it: *Pasta Sciue-Sciue* (pronounced shway-shway). It means pasta in a hurry; that is, in a sauce that you toss together while the pasta cooks.

Roasted red peppers in a jar, fat and juicy; jars of preserved vegetables glistening in their oil; an assortment of olives; cans of pulses – chickpeas, kidney beans, cannellini beans; tomatoes, canned and sun-dried; jars of pestos; a chunk of grating cheese; a string of hot peppers hanging on your wall just waiting to be plucked and tossed into the pot…

Fettuccine al Gorgonzola, Pesto e Mascarpone

Fettuccine with Gorgonzola, Pesto and Mascarpone

This gorgeous creamy pasta is easy to make and is as good eaten cold as it is hot. The pine nuts are not traditional, but they make it so lovely; and if you don't have time to toast them, simple sprinkle them on raw instead. Use a rich and pungent Gorgonzola, or choose any blue cheese you like, and I suggest that garlic-lovers add a little chopped garlic to the cheese and pesto mixture.

SERVES 4–6

4 tablespoons pine nuts or slivered almonds
6–8 tablespoons mascarpone cheese
125g (4½ oz) Gorgonzola cheese, broken or chopped into small pieces
4–6 tablespoons pesto (*see page 19*)
400g (14 oz) fresh fettuccine (flat long ribbons) or 350g (12 oz) dried
Freshly ground black pepper
Sprigs of fresh basil

Lightly toast the pine nuts in a heavy, ungreased frying pan by stirring them about quickly over a medium–high heat until lightly golden and brown in spots. Be careful not to burn them. Then remove from the heat and set aside.

Mash together the mascarpone, Gorgonzola and pesto and set aside while you cook the pasta in a large pan of rapidly boiling salted water until *al dente*. Drain, saving a few spoonfuls of the cooking water.

Toss the pasta with the cheese and pesto mixture, adding the reserved hot cooking water to thin it out a bit. Season with pepper to taste and serve right away, sprinkled with the nuts and basil.

Pasta al Pomodoro e Pesto

Pasta with Tomato Sauce and Pesto

Delicate and buttery, tasting far richer than it really is. Whip it together in moments – the time it takes to gather everything from your shelf.

SERVES 4–6

400g (14 oz) passata (or one of the tomato sauces on pages 17–18)
400g (14 oz) any long flat pasta, such as fettuccine
40–50g (1½–2oz) unsalted butter
125g (4½ oz) pesto (*see page 19*)
3–4 tablespoons freshly grated Parmesan cheese
Salt and freshly ground black pepper

Heat the passata in a pan and set aside while you cook the pasta in a large pan of rapidly boiling salted water until *al dente*. Drain, reserving a few tablespoons of the cooking water, and toss the hot pasta with the tomato sauce. Stir in the butter and some of the hot cooking water, then add the pesto and cheese, stirring in more of the water if the mixture seems dry.

Season to taste, although it may not need salt, then serve up right away, while it is still hot.

Pasta alle Zucchine con Salsa di Peperoni

Pasta with Courgettes and Red-pepper Sauce

This is the lightest, lithest, easiest to prepare and eat pasta imaginable. It also looks very nice, too: pieces of pale courgette, strands of pasta, a red sauce of roasted peppers and the scattering of chopped chives. For a stylish presentation, just sprinkle the chives around the edge of the plate.

SERVES 4

Large jar of roasted red peppers (about 250g/9 oz), or 4 red peppers,
    roasted, seeded and peeled
1 bunch chives, about 25g (1 oz), freshly snipped
2–3 cloves garlic, finely chopped
5–8 leaves basil, thinly sliced
2–3 tablespoons extra virgin olive oil
Dash of balsamic vinegar or white wine vinegar
Salt and freshly ground black pepper
450g (1 lb) spaghetti
4 courgettes, diced or cut into bite-sized pieces

Finely chop the peppers and place them in a bowl with the chives, garlic, basil and half the olive oil. Season to taste with the vinegar, salt and pepper and set aside.

Bring a large pan of salted water to the boil, add the spaghetti and cook for about 4 minutes; add the courgettes and continue to cook until the spaghetti is just tender or *al dente*. Drain, then toss the pasta and courgettes with the remaining olive oil and serve immediately, topping each portion with a dollop of the red-pepper sauce.

Pasta di Mezzanotte
Midnight Pasta

Pasta for a midnight feast, with sweet and fiery peppers and enough garlic to keep away the vampires. Though the recipe serves four, it still works well halved to serve two, or even quartered for a solo bowlful. The sauce can be kept in a tightly covered jar for no longer than two weeks.

SERVES 4

2–5 chillies, chopped (not too hot and fierce)
12 cloves garlic, or more, coarsely chopped
1 red or yellow sweet pepper, seeded and finely chopped
125–175ml (4½–6 fl oz) extra virgin olive oil
450g (1 lb) spaghetti
Salt
1–2 tablespoons freshly chopped parsley

Combine the chillies, garlic and pepper with the olive oil in a heavy saucepan or frying pan and cook over a gentle heat, letting them sizzle, but not really fry, for about 5–8 minutes. You want a spicy oil, rather than a crispy fried mixture.

Meanwhile, cook the spaghetti in a large pan of rapidly boiling salted water, then drain, saving a few tablespoons of the cooking water.

Toss the spaghetti with the pepper sauce and the reserved water, and eat right away in warmed bowls, sprinkled with parsley.

Maccheroni alla Libanese
Small Pasta with Basil, Parsley and Lime

This smart little pasta dish is tangy with lime and fresh with herbs. Eat it as a side dish, alongside a roasted chicken or spicy meat from the barbecue, or serve it for a summer picnic lunch.

SERVES 4–6

4 cloves garlic, finely chopped
3–4 tablespoons extra virgin olive oil
Several large handfuls of sweet basil, roughly torn
350g (12 oz) small macaroni, ditalini or similar (*see pages 11-12*)
3–4 tablespoons freshly chopped parsley
Grated zest of 1 lime
Juice of 2 limes
Salt and freshly ground black pepper or cayenne pepper

Gently heat the garlic in the olive oil in a pan until it just colours lightly and smells fragrant. Remove the pan from the heat and add the basil, which will wilt and go bright green and glossy.

Meanwhile, cook the pasta until *al dente*, then drain, reserving a small spoonful of the cooking liquid.

Toss the hot pasta in the garlic and basil oil, together with the reserved hot cooking water, parsley, grated zest and lime juice. Season with salt and either black or cayenne pepper (or a tiny sprinkling of both) to taste.

Serve up right away, though it's also good eaten at room temperature.

Spaghetti o Trofie con Noci e Parmigiano

Spaghetti or Trofie with Walnuts and Parmesan

Sitting on the warm, sunny terrace of a little seaside café on the Riviera dei Fiori, businessmen at a nearby table discussed the topics of the day and a table of students looked stylish and trendy. My business lunch was with a handsome and charming Italian, and as I tucked into this delicious regional dish I gave only a fleeting thought to my loved ones shivering at home in a London winter.

SERVES 4

400g (14 oz) spaghetti, trofie (corkscrew pasts), or similar (*see page 12*)
4–6 tablespoons extra virgin olive oil
100g (4 oz) walnut pieces, coarsely ground or finely chopped
100g (4 oz) Parmesan cheese, freshly grated
3–5 cloves garlic, finely chopped
Salt and freshly ground black pepper
1 teaspoon lightly crushed fresh thyme or marjoram leaves, or to taste

Cook the spaghetti in a large pan of rapidly boiling salted water until *al dente*.

Meanwhile, in a large bowl, combine the olive oil with the walnuts, cheese, garlic, salt and pepper to taste and thyme or marjoram. Mix well.

Drain the pasta and toss with the sauce, then serve in warmed shallow bowls before it cools.

Conchiglie ai Formaggi

Pasta Shells with Emmenthal and Crème Fraîche

Rugged Swiss-type mountain cheeses are delicious with pasta: so comforting, so delicious and so utterly quick to make. This simple dish is from the Italian Alps – a region you can't help falling in love with.
SERVES 4–6

450g (1 lb) conchiglie (shells)
3 cloves garlic, finely chopped
150g (5 oz) Emmenthal cheese, coarsely grated
100g (4 oz) crème fraîche, or as desired
40–50g (1½ –2oz) butter, or as desired

Cook the pasta in a large pan of rapidly boiling salted water until *al dente*. Drain, reserving a small spoonful of the cooking water, then return the hot pasta to the pan immediately and toss with the rest of the ingredients and the reserved water. If the cheese hasn't melted completely, turn the heat on low and continue to toss until it does. Serve right away.

Spaghetti con Cacio e Pepe
Spaghetti with Cheese and Black Pepper

From the hillside agriturismo *farm hotel of Antico Casale di Scansano, near Scansano in south-west Tuscany, the Pellegrinis serve rustic and irresistible fare such as this traditional pasta. You wouldn't think that something so simple could taste so delicious. Mixing the olive oil, cheese and pepper before tossing it with the pasta ensures an even coating. Use the most gutsy olive oil you can find.*
SERVES 4

400–450g (14 oz–1 lb) spaghetti
250ml (9 fl oz) extra virgin olive oil
100–125g (4–4½ oz) pecorino romano or Parmesan cheese, freshly grated, plus extra for grating at table
1 teaspoon freshly ground black pepper, plus extra for serving

Cook the spaghetti in a large pan of rapidly boiling salted water until *al dente*.

Meanwhile, combine the olive oil with the cheese and pepper. Drain and toss the spaghetti with the oil, cheese and pepper sauce.

Serve immediately in warmed shallow bowls, while it is hot and aromatic. Sprinkle with extra cheese and pepper if desired.

Spaghetti Aglio, Olio e Peperoncino

Spaghetti with Garlic, Oil and Hot Pepper

Cold December, and we trudged the streets of Catania in Sicily in search of a meal and found ourselves at the only open restaurant in town, Il Rapido. 'Special prices for soldiers,' said the very old, faded sign. Nothing had changed in the little restaurant for at least 40 years and our waiter looked as if he had been waiting for us since then. But the food he served was perfection itself – this classic dish of all the poor of southern Italy, garlic and hot pepper spaghetti, is healthy, costs pennies and is blissful to eat.
SERVES 4–6

350–400g (12–14 oz) spaghetti
Salt to taste
100–125ml (4–4½ fl oz) extra virgin olive oil, as desired
1 head of garlic, coarsely chopped (oh, you can use less – but why?)
Several large pinches of dried crumbled red chilli
Freshly grated Parmesan cheese (optional)

Bring a large pan of salted water to the boil and cook the spaghetti until just *al dente*.

Meanwhile, heat the olive oil in a frying pan and cook the garlic with the chilli until just golden. Remove from the heat.

Drain the spaghetti, toss with the hot oil, then serve right away, very hot, with Parmesan if desired.

VARIATION

Spaghetti Aglio, Olio e Alici
Spaghetti with Garlic, Oil and Anchovies

You can decrease the amount of chilli, or omit it entirely. The important thing is to include lots of anchovies, about 10 at least, chopped, and cook them with the garlic and oil. The anchovies will melt, creating a garlicky, briny oil to toss with the pasta and some chopped parsley and freshly ground black pepper to taste, and yummmmm… no cheese, please!

Pasta allo Zafferano e Rucola

Tuscan Pasta with Saffron and Rocket

This is the instant dish of my friend Monica Panerai of Florence, the one she whips up for both company and comfort. Monica works for the Comune della Toscana *(town council) and is one of the most helpful souls I know and a wonderful guide to her region.*

Adding saffron to pasta is traditional in the little town of San Gimignano, where the orange sachets can be seen for sale everywhere. Be sure to use wild rocket rather than the blander cultivated variety.

SERVES 4–6

Several pinches of saffron threads
4–6 tablespoons extra virgin olive oil
500g (1 lb 2 oz) shortish tube-shaped pasta such as fat ditali, penne or
    rigatoni
2 cloves garlic, finely chopped
100g (4 oz) wild rocket leaves, coarsely chopped
4–6 tablespoons freshly grated Parmesan or aged pecorino cheese, or as
    desired
Salt and freshly ground black pepper

Lightly toast the saffron threads in a heavy, ungreased frying pan and gently crush them with a fork or spoon. Remove from the heat, pour in the olive oil and leave to macerate.

Meanwhile, in a large pan of rapidly boiling salted water, cook the pasta according to its size and shape; use the packet as a guideline. When *al dente*, drain and reserve a few tablespoons of the cooking water to add to the sauce.

Toss the hot pasta with the saffron oil (I do it in the frying pan in which the saffron was toasted), then mix in the reserved cooking water with the garlic, rocket and finally the cheese. Season to taste and serve right away.

Penne con Zucchine

Penne with Courgettes, Carbonara-style

This is not a pretty dish, but it is extremely comforting and delicious, and quick to whip up after a long evening out when you want a little something to cosy up to.
SERVES 4–6

3 tablespoons or more extra virgin olive oil
4 small-to-medium courgettes, shredded or grated over the large holes of a
   grater
5 cloves garlic, chopped
350–400g (12–14 oz) penne (quills)
2–3 eggs, lightly beaten
175g (6 oz) fontina or similar cheese, diced
100g (4 oz) Parmesan cheese, freshly grated
Salt and freshly ground black pepper
10 or more sprigs fresh basil, shredded

Heat a little of the olive oil in a large frying pan and, when it is very hot, quickly cook the courgettes until they are limp and lightly browned in spots. Remove them from the pan and turn down the heat. Add the remaining olive oil and the garlic and warm through for a few moments until fragrant but not browned. Remove from the heat.

Meanwhile, cook the penne in a large pan of rapidly boiling salted water until *al dente*, then drain, reserving a few spoonfuls of the pasta cooking water (though you might not need it as the courgettes become juicy when they cook).

Toss the hot pasta into the pan of garlic and olive oil along with the courgettes, egg and two cheeses. Combine well, then return the pan to the heat for a moment or two, tossing all the while to allow the egg to cook and form a cloak evenly around the pasta. If the mixture is dry, add a few spoonfuls of the pasta cooking liquid to the pan, and continue to toss over the heat.

Season to taste and sprinkle on the basil. Serve right away.

Spaghettini ai Pomodori Secchi
Thin Spaghetti with Sun-dried Tomatoes

Last winter I found myself in deepest Sicily with about 100 olive growers to celebrate the harvest. We watched traditional dances, heard songs of the olive harvest, trekked through olive groves and ate good food. I loved the Sicilian way of serving sun-dried tomatoes, tender and succulent, and topped with crisp breadcrumbs. Here I've turned it into a pasta dish, with the crumbs and a little of the cooking liquid forming the sauce, along with the heady olive oil.
SERVES 4–6

About 100ml (4 fl oz) extra virgin olive oil, more if needed
5–8 heaped tablespoons dried breadcrumbs (prepared from good bread)
6–8 cloves garlic, coarsely chopped
About 20 sun-dried (dry, not marinated) tomatoes
400g (14 oz) spaghettini
Salt and freshly ground black pepper
Several pinches of oregano leaves, crushed

Heat half the olive oil in a frying pan until it is smoking hot, then reduce the heat to medium–low and add the crumbs. Stir them around until they are lightly golden-brown and crispy. Add the garlic, remove from the pan and set aside.

Using scissors, cut the sun-dried tomatoes into strips. Add them to a large pan of salted water (but don't add salt if the tomatoes themselves are already salted) and bring to the boil. Add the pasta to the boiling water and cook until *al dente*.

Drain, reserving about 125ml (4½ fl oz) of the cooking water. Toss the pasta in the frying pan with the remaining olive oil, salt and plenty of black pepper to taste, oregano leaves and as much of the cooking liquid to keep it all supple, slippery and lightly sauced. Toss in the crumbs and serve right away.

Pasta Fredda alla Giudea
Cold Pasta for Shabbat

Cold pasta was never really part of the Italian table, until the rest of the country discovered the dishes created for Shabbat, *the Sabbath, by the Italian Jewish community, whose meals had to be made in advance and were not permitted to be reheated.*

A simple dish from Florence, this is a terrific accompaniment to a saucy stew on a hot summer's day. Instead of mild roasted peppers, you can add a bit of hot Tuscan peperoncino flakes.

SERVES 4–6

250g (9 oz) dried egg pasta, such as tagliatelli
2–4 tablespoons extra virgin olive oil
3 cloves garlic, finely chopped
4–6 tablespoons coarsely chopped fresh parsley
1 roasted red pepper from a jar, chopped
About 20 green olives, stoned and coarsely chopped or slivered

Cook the pasta in a large pan of boiling salted water until *al dente*, or as directed on the packet. Drain, rinse in cold water and toss with the olive oil, garlic, parsley, red pepper and olives. Serve cold.

VARIATION

Pasta Fredda con Melanzane
Cold Pasta with Aubergine

Add cold, bite-sized cubes of an aubergine fried in olive oil when you toss in the other ingredients. Aubergine, roasted peppers, garlic and olive oil are quintessential Italian-Jewish ingredients, as are artichokes.

Spaghetti con Alici

Spaghetti with Anchovies and Breadcrumbs

This simple dish comes from Naples: it is truly cucina povera *(cooking of the poor) for its ingredients are humble indeed: and nothing could be more delicious.*
SERVES 4–6

15 cloves garlic, coarsely chopped
Several pinches of crumbled dried chilli
125ml (4½ fl oz) extra virgin olive oil
6 anchovies, chopped
400g (14 oz) spaghetti
2–3 tablespoons toasted breadcrumbs

Heat the garlic and chilli with the olive oil in a large pan, then add the anchovies and cook together over a medium–low heat, stirring, until the anchovies just melt. Set aside while you cook the spaghetti in a large pan of rapidly boiling salted water, until *al dente*. Drain, reserving a spoonful or two of the cooking liquid.

Toss the hot drained pasta with the flavoured pepper oil and the cooking liquid, then stir in the breadcrumbs. Serve up right away.

Big Baked Panfuls

A big sizzling pan emerges from the oven, its top layer lightly browned, juices bubbling up around the edge, oozing their irresistible lusty perfume.

Baked pasta is festive food, a hearty dish meaning generous portions. It's a big deal of a dish because a baked pasta takes time and care to put together. But it is worth it: cut into the casserole and savour the textures of the crisp outer layer, the tender inner layer and the sensuous pooling of sauce…

It can also be elegant fare, such as the creamy Lasagne Bianco I forked up in Spoleto not long ago. Or it can be as cosy as macaroni cheese with a zesty beetroot relish.

Stuffing pasta, wrapping it around fillings, layering it with sauces, all that rolling and folding – invite your friends and make a day of it; there's nothing like being busy in the kitchen together to catch up on all the news.

These dishes are great for large groups – most can be multiplied – as they can be done ahead of time then popped into the oven, leaving you to enjoy your guests.

Anelli al Forno

Pasta Rings Baked with Peas, Meat and Cheese

This Sicilian dish is traditionally made with a big meaty ragù, *simmered until tender. If you have some delicious Sicilian sausages, add those to the sauce in place of, or as well as, the minced beef.*

SERVES 4–6

2–3 tablespoons extra virgin olive oil
1 large onion, finely chopped
500g (1 lb 2 oz) minced beef or other meat
125ml (4½ fl oz) dry white wine
3–5 cloves garlic, thinly sliced
3 tablespoons tomato purée
250ml (9 fl oz) stock, or half stock and half water
400g (14 oz) fresh, young shelled or frozen peas
Handful of basil leaves, roughly torn
500g (1 lb 2 oz) anelli, or small, ring-shaped pasta
8–10 tablespoons home-made dried breadcrumbs
100g (4 oz) Parmesan or pecorino cheese, freshly grated
400g (14 oz) assiago or fresh cheese such as fresh pecorino, diced

Preheat the oven to 190°C/375°F/Gas 5.

In a large pan, heat a tablespoon or so of the olive oil and lightly sauté the onion and brown the meat in spots, then add the wine and garlic and simmer until the wine has almost all evaporated. Add the tomato purée and stock and simmer for 20 minutes or so, until the mixture has thickened and developed a good flavour. Stir in the peas and basil, season to taste and set aside.

Cook the pasta in a large pan of rapidly boiling salted water until almost *al dente*. Drain and set aside.

Drizzle about half the remaining oil in the bottom of a 3 litre (5¼ pint) soufflé dish, then sprinkle with half the breadcrumbs. Layer in the pasta, *ragù* and cheeses, ending with some cheese. Finish with the remaining breadcrumbs and drizzle the rest of the olive oil over the top. Bake for about 20 minutes or until the top is lightly crispy. Serve right away.

Cannelloni all'Aeoliana

Cannelloni Filled with Spinach and Ricotta, Baked with Tomatoes and Basil

From one of the group of islands known as the Aeolian Islands off the coast of Sicily, this dish of tender pasta captures the intense flavour of the Mediterranean. It tastes so vivacious and bright, yet light, like the most delicate lasagne you could imagine. I've added spinach to the filling, though it's still delicious without. Unlike most dishes on my table, this one is sauced without garlic – just the pure flavour of tomatoes and basil.

SERVES 4

300g (11 oz) fresh pasta sheets, home-made (*see page 14*) or bought, about
    the size of lasagne, or wonton wrappers from Oriental shops
800g (1¾ lb) fresh spinach leaves
250g (9 oz) ricotta cheese
Nutmeg for grating
125g (4½ oz) mozzarella cheese, diced
1 egg, lightly beaten
75g (3 oz) or several handfuls of freshly grated Parmesan or pecorino
    cheese, plus a little extra if desired
Salt and freshly ground black pepper
400g (14 oz) canned tomatoes or fresh ripe tomatoes, chopped
2 tablespoons tomato purée
3 tablespoons extra virgin olive oil
Several handfuls fresh basil leaves, torn or thinly sliced

Preheat the oven to 190°C/375°F/Gas 5.

    If using fresh pasta, parboil the sheets in a large pan of rapidly boiling salted water until about half tender, then submerge in cold water, to stop them cooking, while you make the filling. If using egg-roll wrappers do not precook, as they are very thin and will cook with the juices of the tomatoes during baking.

    Cook the spinach for a few minutes in a large pan over a medium heat with a few tablespoons of water, tightly covered, until the leaves are limp and just bright green. Remove from the heat and leave to cool, before draining, squeezing dry and chopping coarsely.

In a bowl, combine the spinach with the ricotta, grated nutmeg to taste, mozzarella, egg and half the Parmesan. Season to taste.

In another bowl mix the chopped tomatoes with the tomato purée and spread half of this sauce over the bottom of a large baking pan of at least 30 x 25 x 5cm (12 x 10 x 2 in).

If you have parboiled the pasta, drain for a moment on a cloth. Taking one sheet of pasta or one wonton wrapper at a time, spoon a generous amount of the spinach mixture on to one-quarter of it. Roll up and place on top of the tomato sauce. Repeat until the pasta and filling are used up, then top with the remaining tomato sauce and cheese, drizzle with olive oil and bake for about 20 minutes, or until it is sizzling and flecked golden on top.

Serve sprinkled with the basil and some extra Parmesan if desired.

VARIATION

Cannelloni Terrestri
Cannelloni with Meat and Spinach Filling

A delicious filling if you've any left-over roast such as beef or veal.

Omit the mozzarella and decrease the amount of ricotta to 2–3 tablespoons, or substitute with the same amount of cream or crème fraîche.

In a frying pan, sauté ½ a chopped onion and a chopped carrot in a little olive oil until softened, add the finely chopped or shredded cooked left-over meat (about 250g/9oz) and brown together. Pour a glass of dry white wine into the pan, turn up the heat and simmer until it evaporates, then add any of the pan juices left over from the roast, with the fat removed, or a glass of stock. Continue cooking over a high heat until it has reduced to only a few tablespoons of strong-flavoured sauce.

Combine the meat and contents of the pan with the cooked spinach and enough of the ricotta or cream to bind it, along with the raw egg etc. Continue the recipe as above.

Instead of cannelloni, use orecchiette grandi, the huge ear-shaped pastas of Puglia, for stuffing.

Pasticcio di Ravioli al Rosmarino

Baked Ravioli with Rosemary-tomato Sauce

A baked casserole of layered ravioli, sauce and cheese is as lusty and flavourful as any lasagne, and so easy to make – a delicious cheat! Use any filled pasta as long as it's a good one – I prefer ravioli. Many supermarket brands are too stodgy and un-Italian-tasting.

With cheese-filled ravioli, I add meatballs or some browned minced beef to the layers; with a meat filling, I add dollops of ricotta cheese. However, you don't need to add either for the dish still to be delicious.

SERVES 4

450–500g (1 lb–1 lb 2oz) ravioli stuffed with spinach, meat or cheese
Salt and freshly ground black pepper
400g (14 oz) fresh or canned tomatoes, chopped
Several sprigs of fresh, tender rosemary leaves, removed from stems and
    chopped
3–5 cloves garlic, finely chopped
2–3 tablespoons extra virgin olive oil
250g (9 oz) meltable cheese, such as mozzarella or fontina, chopped
50g (2 oz) or more Parmesan cheese, freshly grated
250g (9 oz) minced meat, browned in a pan or made into tiny meatballs
    (optional)
250g (9 oz) ricotta cheese (optional)

Preheat the oven to 190°C/375°F/Gas 5.

Cook the ravioli in a large pan of rapidly boiling salted water until not quite *al dente*; undercook slightly because they will be cooking some more in the oven. Drain and set aside. Purée the tomatoes with their juices.

In a 20cm (8 in) or so casserole, layer the ravioli with the tomato, seasoning, rosemary, garlic, a drizzle of olive oil, a scattering of mozzarella or fontina and Parmesan, adding the browned minced meat, meatballs or dollops of ricotta along the way if you choose.

Finish the dish with a layer of cheeses and a drizzle of olive oil, then bake for 15–20 minutes or until the cheese topping has melted and is sizzling and lightly browned in spots. Raise the heat for 5 minutes or so at the end if necessary.

Cannelloni alla Pesaro

Cannelloni Filled with Turkey, Chicken Liver and Ham

On a visit to Pesaro, near Venice, I was thrilled to find this cannelloni dish. Filled with a rich mixture of turkey (or chicken), chicken liver, prosciutto and salami, oh, and – how could I forget? – a handful of wild mushrooms, it is divine. The large cannelloni tubes are easy to fill using a teaspoon rather than piping bag so you can have a nice chunky mixture. And you can let it all bake together without cooking the pasta first.

SERVES 4–6

250g (9 oz) fresh pasta sheets *(see page 14)* or dried cannelloni tubes
250g (9 oz) cheese such as fontina, Gruyère or other mild but flavourful
    melting cheese, coarsely grated

For the béchamel sauce
40g (1½ oz) unsalted butter
3 tablespoons flour
450ml (16 fl oz) milk
Salt and freshly ground black pepper
Nutmeg for grating

For the filling
175g (6 oz) chicken or turkey breast, cut into bite-sized pieces
2 chicken livers, cut into several pieces
125g (4½ oz) prosciutto or mixture of prosciutto and salami, cut up or
    coarsely chopped
1 medium-to-large onion, finely chopped
1 tablespoon extra virgin olive oil or 15g (½ oz) butter
250ml (9 fl oz) dry white wine
Handful of dried mixed mushrooms, broken up into small pieces
350ml (12 fl oz) stock, preferably mushroom, such as the Italian porcini
    stock cube or bottled concentrated chicken stock mixed with water

Preheat the oven to 200°C/400°F/Gas 6.

If using fresh pasta, parboil the sheets in a large pan of rapidly boiling salted water until about half tender. Submerge in cold water, to stop them cooking, while you make the filling.

To make the béchamel sauce, melt the butter in a small saucepan, sprinkle in the flour and cook for a few minutes, stirring, then remove from the heat and add the milk all at once. Stir vigorously with a wooden spoon or a balloon whisk, then return to the heat and cook, still stirring, over a medium heat until the mixture thickens – you want quite a thick sauce. Remove from the heat and season with salt, pepper and lots of grated nutmeg to taste. Set aside.

To make the filling, mince the meat, chicken liver and prosciutto (or prosciutto and salami) in a food processor until it is almost a purée. Lightly sauté the onion in the olive oil or butter in a frying pan until it is softened, then add the meat mixture and brown it in spots over a medium–high heat, stirring until it forms a chunky, textured mix.

Pour in the wine and cook over a high heat for about 5 minutes or until it has reduced. Add the mushrooms with about a third of the stock and continue to cook over a high heat for a few minutes or long enough to meld the flavours and reduce it just a little. The mushroom pieces will plump up, too. Then stir in about a third of the béchamel sauce, which might have become clumpy and thick but that's fine – you want it to hold the filling together.

To stuff the cannelloni, hold a pasta tube upright and, using a teaspoon, drop the filling into the tube, then lay it down in a large baking dish. Repeat until all of the filling and pasta is used; if you have any filling left, just spoon it around the stuffed cannelloni. If using fresh pasta sheets, roll them around some filling and place, seam-side down, in the dish.

Pour the remaining stock over the dish and dollop the rest of the béchamel randomly over the cannelloni. Sprinkle with the cheese, cover with foil and bake for 25–30 minutes. Remove the foil and return to the oven for another 10 minutes to allow the top to sizzle and lightly brown. Remove and leave it to sit for another 10 minutes before serving.

Conchiglie con Pollo Arrosto

Shell Pasta with Roasted Chicken

I love Sunday lunches in Italy, hours spent with the whole family (even if it's someone else's family) gathered round a table heaped with wonderful food; everyone fussing over the baby. This big ol' panful of pasta, tossed into the pan juices of a roast chicken, with tomatoes and grilled aubergine, makes great Sunday-lunch fare. It's a delicious example of a piatto unico, *or one-pan plate – the pasta is the first course and the chicken – with salad – the main. Here I serve them together, though.*
SERVES 4–6

1 medium-sized chicken, about 1–1.6 kg (2¼–3½ lb)
Large head of garlic, divided into cloves, unpeeled
Salt and freshly ground black pepper
3 tablespoons extra virgin olive oil
1–2 tablespoons balsamic vinegar
2–3 tablespoons pastis or anisette
1–2 teaspoons dried Italian mixed herbs or good Italian oregano
½ onion (or several spring onions, bent in half to fit into the chicken)
1 wedge of lemon, preferably unwaxed and organic
1 aubergine, sliced
400g (14 oz) canned chopped tomatoes
Small pinch of sugar, if needed
350g (12 oz) conchiglie (shells), or similar

Preheat the oven to 180°C/350°F/Gas 4. Rub the chicken with half a peeled garlic clove, salt and pepper, olive oil (reserve a little to brush on to the aubergine), balsamic vinegar, pastis and herbs. Into its cavity place the onion, a few whole garlic cloves and a wedge of lemon.

Place the chicken on its side in a roasting pan that just fits it with a few more garlic cloves around it and roast for about 20 minutes. Turn it on to its other side for a further 20 minutes, then on its back to brown the top for another 15–20 minutes.

Meanwhile, brush the aubergine slices with the remaining olive oil and grill on each side until lightly browned and tender, about 10 minutes. Set aside.

Remove the chicken from the oven when it is cooked – the juices will run clear when a skewer is inserted into the thickest part of the bird – and set it on a platter. Discard the onion, garlic and lemon in the cavity, reserving any juices that escape. Cut the chicken into portions, cover with foil and keep warm.

Skim off the fat from the chicken juices in the pan, then add the remaining garlic cloves, peeled and chopped, and the tomatoes. Stir through, then pour the reserved escaped juices from the chicken into the tomato mixture, too. Keep stirring to spoon up all the delicious roasty bits left at the bottom of the pan.

Pour the mixture into a saucepan and on a high heat simmer it down, by about a third, to a thick flavoursome sauce then turn down the heat. Check the seasoning and add a tiny bit of sugar if the tomatoes are acidic.

Meanwhile, cook the pasta in a large pan of rapidly boiling salted water until *al dente*. Toss it with half the tomato sauce and the aubergine and top with the chicken. Serve it immediately, with the rest of the sauce over the chicken.

Lasagne alla Veneziana

Lasagne with Peas, Tomato Sauce and Béchamel

The canals steamed in the shimmering heat as I wandered through Venice. I longed for romance, but got this great recipe instead.

Peas are a hallmark of the region. Beautiful and delicious, they pop up in many local dishes: stewed with veal, stirred into risotto, simmered with fish or tossed into pasta. Here, they are layered with lasagne, béchamel and tomato sauce – a more luscious, enticing party piece I doubt you will find.

SERVES 8–10

2 kg (4½ lb) fresh spinach pasta (green) in wide noodles or cut into
  lasagne sheets, or 700g (1½ lb) dried lasagne, either all green or a
  combination of green and white
250–350g (9–12 oz) shelled fresh or frozen young peas
300g (11 oz) Parmesean cheese, freshly grated
350g (12 oz) mozzarella, fontina, or other creamy meltable cheese
2 tablespoons extra virgin olive oil
½ teaspoon dried oregano, crushed between the fingers

For the béchamel sauce
50g (2oz) unsalted butter
3 heaped tablespoons flour
750ml (27 fl oz) milk (semi-skimmed is fine)
Large pinch of freshly grated nutmeg
Salt and freshly ground black pepper

For the tomato sauce
1 medium–large or 2 medium–small onions, finely chopped
3 cloves garlic, finely chopped
1 smallish carrot, finely chopped
2 tablespoons freshly chopped parsley

2 tablespoons extra virgin olive oil
½–1 teaspoon fennel seeds, or to taste
½ teaspoon dried marjoram, thyme, rosemary, or other Italian herb, or a
**   mixture**
3 cans (400g/14 oz each) chopped tomatoes
4 heaped tablespoons tomato purée
½ teaspoon sugar, or to taste
Salt and freshly ground black pepper

Preheat the oven to 190°C/375°F/Gas 5.

To make the béchamel sauce, melt the butter in a heavy saucepan, then sprinkle in the flour. Stir over a medium–low heat to make a roux. Do not allow it to burn or brown. Take off the heat and add the milk all at once, stirring well with a wooden spoon or a balloon whisk to a smooth sauce. Sprinkle in the nutmeg, salt and pepper, then return to the heat and continue to stir over a medium–high heat until it comes to the boil. Reduce the heat to low and allow the sauce to simmer for 10 minutes or so, stirring all the while, until it has thickened. If it is lumpy at this stage, either whisk it with a balloon whisk or whirl it in a food processor or blender. Set it aside.

To make the tomato sauce, sauté the onion, garlic, carrot and parsley in the olive oil in another pan for a few minutes until the onion is soft. Add the rest of the sauce ingredients and simmer for 10 minutes or until the mixture is well flavoured.

Assemble the lasagne in a large ovenproof dish, about 35 x 25 x 7.5cm (14 x 10 x 3 in). First spread several tablespoons of tomato sauce over the bottom of the dish, then place in a layer of pasta sheets. If you are using dried lasagne, you may have to precook it first (follow the instructions on the packet).

Top with about 250ml (9 fl oz) béchamel sauce followed by about half the peas, then about a third of both the cheeses together.

Top with another layer of pasta, more tomato sauce and more of the cheese, then another layer of pasta, the rest of the béchamel sauce, peas and another third of the cheeses, then layer on the rest of the pasta and tomato sauce, finishing with the cheeses. Drizzle with olive oil and sprinkle oregano over the top.

Cover tightly with foil and bake for about 15 minutes, then uncover and bake for another 10–15 minutes, until the cheese is bubbly and lightly browned. Serve immediately.

Timballi di Melanzane con Ditalini

Aubergine Turbans Filled with Ditalini

Fresh autumnal herbs such as sage, rosemary, marjoram or oregano add their perfume to this lusty dish from Italy's sun-drenched south. Make the turbans of aubergine-wrapped pasta and cheese either in ramekins or in one big robust casserole.

Though traditionally prepared using smoked mozzarella or provolone, I also like it with a fresher-tasting cheese and sometimes include a dollop of goat's cheese. Serve it with a mound of grilled Italian sausages.

SERVES 4–6

2 large aubergines, sliced very thinly lengthways
2 tablespoons extra virgin olive oil, plus a little extra for frying
1 onion, finely chopped
3–4 cloves garlic, finely chopped
400g (14 oz) crushed or chopped fresh or canned tomatoes
4–5 tablespoons tomato purée
Salt and freshly ground black pepper
Several sprigs each of fresh sage, rosemary and marjoram or oregano,
    leaves removed and chopped, reserving a few sprigs for garnish
400g (14 oz) ditalini or other small macaroni pasta (*see pages 11-12*)
175g–200g (6–7 oz) frozen or blanched shelled fresh young peas
350g (12 oz) fontina, mozzarella, provolone or a mixture of melting
    cheeses, diced
50g (2 oz) or more asiago, pecorino or Parmesan cheese, freshly grated

Preheat the oven to 180°C/350°F/Gas 4.

Brown the aubergine slices in a little olive oil in a large frying pan. When each slice is supple and browned in places, place on absorbent paper. Put the 2 tablespoons of olive oil into the pan and lightly sauté the onion and garlic until softened, then add the tomatoes and tomato purée. Cook over a medium–high heat until the mixture has thickened, then season with salt and pepper and add the herbs. Set aside.

Bring a large pan of salted water to the boil and cook the ditalini until *al dente*, then drain. Combine the pasta with the sauce, peas and cheeses.

Line ramekins or an oiled, round and ovenproof 3 litre (5¼ pint) mould, such as a soufflé dish, with two-thirds of the aubergine slices. Spoon the pasta mixed with the cheeses into the centre and cover the top with the remaining aubergine. Pat down firmly and bake for 30–40 minutes. Remove from the oven and leave to settle for 5–10 minutes.

Loosen the edges of the ramekins or mould with a knife and invert the turbans on to serving plates or a dish. Garnish with sprigs of herbs and serve any left-over sauce spooned around it.

Lasagne Bianche alla Spoleto

Lasagne with Béchamel, Cheese, Vegetables and Prosciutto

Lasagne Bianche *is a speciality of Spoleto, a tiny town in the mountains above Rome that really likes its food and produces excellent olive oil. A Roman city which fought off Hannibal and his elephants on their way to Rome and once had Lucrezia Borgia as its first lady, Spoleto is now most famous for its summer music festival. Here you can savour this luscious layering of lasagne, Parmesan, peas and ham. I use cannelloni as they seem to be thinner than commercial lasagne, or you could make some delicate home-rolled lasagne.*

SERVES 4–6

300g (11 oz) dried lasagne or cannelloni or 350g (12 oz) fresh
Salt
Extra virgin olive oil
2 cloves garlic, halved
2 courgettes, diced
125ml (4 fl oz) dry white wine
100g (4 oz) prosciutto, shredded
About 100g (4 oz) Parmesan cheese
75–100g (3–4 oz) tiny shelled peas, either fresh and blanched or frozen

For the béchamel sauce
50g (2oz) butter
4 tablespoons flour
570ml (1 pint) milk
250ml (9 fl oz) chicken stock
Salt
A small pinch of cayenne
Nutmeg for grating
1 egg yolk, lightly beaten

Preheat the oven to 200°C/400°F/Gas 6.

Cook the lasagne or cannelloni in a large pan of rapidly boiling salted water until not quite *al dente*. Drain carefully and immerse the pasta in cold water, then lightly drain and set aside, tossed lightly with a little olive oil. If using cannelloni cut the cooked tubes into flat squares before tossing them in oil.

For the béchamel, in a heavy saucepan melt the butter until it foams then sprinkle in the flour. Cook until it goes slightly golden then stir and cook for a few more minutes, removing it from the heat before it browns. Pour in the milk all at once and stir well with a wooden spoon or balloon whisk. Return the pan to the heat and continue to cook over a medium–low heat, stirring continuously as it starts to thicken. After 5 minutes or so, remove it from the heat, stir in the chicken stock and mix well until smooth. Season with the salt, cayenne and nutmeg, and stir in the egg, taking care not to let it curdle. Set aside.

In a sauté pan, gently heat 2 tablespoons of the olive oil and stir in the garlic. Add the courgettes and sauté until they are tender and lightly browned in spots. Remove any garlic that threatens to brown or burn. Pour in the wine and turn the heat up high and simmer until the wine has reduced to a few tablespoons. Remove from the heat and stir in the prosciutto.

Spread a spoonful of the béchamel sauce over the bottom of a greased 35 x 28 x 5cm (14 x 11 x 2 in) ovenproof baking dish and sprinkle with some of the Parmesan. Follow with a layer of pasta. Top with more béchamel and about half the courgette mixture, then more Parmesan and another layer of pasta. Pour on some more béchamel, then sprinkle the peas over, more Parmesan and the rest of the pasta followed by the remaining courgette mixture and béchamel. Sprinkle the remaining Parmesan over the top.

Cover with foil and bake for 10–15 minutes, then remove the foil and bake for a further 10–15 minutes or until the top is golden and crispy in places and creamy beneath.

Pasta al Forno con Formaggio

Baked Pasta and Cheeses with Beetroot Pesto

There are fewer dishes more appealing or homely than a casserole of macaroni and cheese: crusty on the top with crumbs and gratinéed cheese, creamy and gooey inside .
  This dish has a secret fashion accessory, however – a dollop of tangy beetroot pesto to serve alongside. Beetroot and pesto are a delicious if very unorthodox combination, and the little relish lifts the cheesy pasta casserole delightfully.
SERVES 4–6

450g (1 lb) macaroni or other chunky pasta such as farfalle, elbows, shells
  or penne (quills)
50g (2oz) butter
2 tablespoons flour
500ml (18 fl oz) hot milk
2 cloves garlic, chopped
Salt and pepper
Small pinch cayenne
Nutmeg for grating
400g (14 oz) sharp cheese such as Cheddar or young pecorino, grated
175g (6 oz) blue cheese such as Gorgonzola, crumbled
50–75g (2–3 oz) Parmesan, pecorino or similar cheese, freshly grated
2 tablespoons fresh or dried breadcrumbs

For the beetroot pesto
4 cooked beetroots, peeled and diced
Few drops of balsamic or white wine vinegar
2–3 tablespoons pesto (*see page 19*)

Preheat the oven to 200°C/400°F/Gas 6.
  Cook the macaroni in a large pan of rapidly boiling salted water until not quite *al dente*, then drain and set aside.
  In a saucepan, melt half the butter until it foams and turns lightly golden, sprinkle in the flour and cook, stirring, for a moment or two taking care not to brown it. Remove from the heat and add the milk all at once, stirring briskly with a wooden spoon, then return to the heat and continue to cook, stirring, until the sauce thickens. Stir in the garlic, salt and pepper to taste, the cayenne and grate in some nutmeg.
  Toss the pasta with the sauce and cheeses (reserving some of the sharp cheese and Parmesan), then pour it into a casserole and sprinkle the top with the remaining cheeses and breadcrumbs. Dot with the remaining butter and bake for about 30 minutes or until the top of the casserole turns crusty and golden.
  Meanwhile toss the beetroot with the vinegar and let it sit for a few minutes before mixing with the pesto. Serve each portion of creamy macaroni and crusty topping with a spoonful of the beetroot pesto alongside.

Pasta con Cavolfiore e Ricotta
Baked Macaroni with Cauliflower and Ricotta

Though this traditional Sicilian country dish calls for cauliflower, it often refers to broccoli or Roman broccoli, which has a pointed heart. If you can find it, use it in this dish, it's delicious.
SERVES 4–6

1 kg (2¼ lb) cauliflower, broccoli or Roman broccoli, or a mixture, cut into bite-sized chunks
2–3 eggs, lightly beaten
Nutmeg for grating
150g (5 oz) Parmesan cheese, freshly grated
Salt and freshly ground black pepper
3 tablespoons or more extra virgin olive oil
3–4 cloves garlic, thinly sliced
500g (1 lb 2 oz) macaroni, or other similar chunky pasta
500g (1 lb 2 oz) ricotta cheese

Preheat the oven to 190°C/375°F/Gas 5.

Cook the cauliflower and/or broccoli in a pan of rapidly boiling salted water until just tender. Drain, saving the cooking water for the pasta, and allow the vegetables to cool.

Meanwhile, combine the eggs, some grated nutmeg, Parmesan, salt and pepper in a bowl and set aside.

In another pan, gently heat the olive oil and cook the garlic until just lightly golden. Remove from the pan (Italians might throw the garlic away; I never do – I eat it on bread, or add it to the sauce). Stir the cauliflower into the garlic-flavoured oil, breaking it up as it cooks, so that it absorbs the oil well.

Bring the reserved vegetable cooking water to a rapid boil and cook the pasta until it is not quite *al dente*. Drain and toss the pasta with the ricotta, then layer it in a 3 litre (5¼ pint) soufflé dish with the cauliflower and the egg mixture, ending with the last of the egg mixture poured over the top.

Bake for about 40 minutes, or until a golden crust forms.

Stuffed Pasta and Gnocchi

Ravioli, tortellini, agnolotti, caramelle, panzerotti – the list goes on and on. All are types of pasta that can be filled with a variety of vegetables, herbs, seafood, meats and cheeses.

Fresh pasta is straightforward to make (see pages 14–16). You can make a big wad of dough and keep it in the freezer to roll out when you need it. However, if you're short of time, you can use wonton wrappers, available from oriental food shops, to make quickly prepared and delicious little ravioli or dumplings.

You can make pasta with an almost stained–glass appearance by sandwiching a herb between two squares of pasta or wonton. Place a fragrant basil leaf, or fresh flat-leaf parsley leaf, or petals of edible flowers, such as nasturtiums, on a square of thinly rolled-out dough, brush the edges with water, seal another piece over it and roll it flat. A quick boil, and what emerges from the pan is tender and translucent, the herb imbedded in the pasta, pretty as a picture and fragrant, too.

Cannelloni di Ricotta in Salsa di Peperoni con Tartufo

Pasta Tubes Filled with Ricotta, in a Spicy Red-pepper Sauce with Truffle

Apart from cannelloni tubes, this elegantly flavoured dish can be made with any ricotta-filled pasta, or you can use wonton wrappers or home-made pasta to encase the ricotta.

SERVES 4

For the cannelloni
12–16 cannelloni tubes
Salt and freshly ground black pepper
300–350g (11–12 oz) ricotta cheese
125g (4½ oz) Parmesan cheese, freshly grated
2 egg yolks
Nutmeg for grating
A drizzle of truffle oil
Butter for dotting the top of the dish

For the red-pepper sauce
1 red pepper, seeded and thinly sliced
1 onion, thinly sliced
2–3 tablespoons extra virgin olive oil
5 cloves garlic, coarsely chopped
1 dried hot chilli pepper, broken up into small pieces
Pinch of cayenne or other hot-pepper flavouring (optional)
400g (14 oz) fresh or canned tomatoes, chopped
Salt and freshly ground black pepper
Pinch of sugar if needed

Preheat the oven to 180°C/350°F/Gas 4.

To make the sauce, in a large pan lightly sauté the pepper and onion in the olive oil over a low heat until they are soft. Add the garlic, hot pepper and cayenne (if using) and cook for a further 5 minutes or so. Stir in the tomatoes and cook over a medium–high heat until you have a thick, sauce-like mixture. Season to taste, adding a pinch of sugar if necessary. Stew together for a few minutes longer.

Meanwhile, parboil the cannelloni in rapidly boiling salted water for 3–4 minutes until they are half cooked. Drain and place in cold water while you make the filling.

In a bowl, combine the ricotta with all except 2–3 tablespoons of the Parmesan, then add the egg yolks, some grated nutmeg, a drizzle of truffle oil and salt and pepper to taste.

Spread the red-pepper sauce on to the bottom of a 35 x 28 x 5cm (14 x 11 x 2 in) baking dish. Drain the pasta and pat dry on a clean tea-cloth, then stuff the cheese mixture evenly into the tubes. Arrange them on top of the sauce in the baking dish.

Dot the top of the cannelloni with butter, sprinkle with the remaining Parmesan and cover the dish loosely with foil. Bake for 20–25 minutes, then remove the foil for a further 10 minutes or until the top is brown and crispy.

Serve right away, sizzling in the dish.

Ravioli di Zucca alla Mantovana con Salvia

Pumpkin Ravioli with Butter, Sage and Parmesan

Pumpkin ravioli is a speciality of Mantova, in northern Italy, an heirloom of the once thriving Jewish community. In fact, the pumpkin is said to have been brought to Italy by Jews fleeing from Spain during the Inquisition.

In this dish the ravioli, stuffed with pumpkin and ricotta, are served with lashings of sage butter, pine nuts and Parmesan. You can serve them too with a gingery tomato sauce (see page 180), or a light, creamy cloak (see page 134).
SERVES 4

32–48 pasta rounds (about 6cm/2½ in diameter), gyoza or wonton pasta
   squares, or as many as necessary
85–100g (3–4oz) unsalted butter, or as desired
Handful of fresh young flavourful sage leaves
Extra grated Parmesan or asiago cheese
1–2 tablespoons pine nuts, raw or lightly toasted

For the pumpkin filling
500–600g (around 1¼ lb) pumpkin, preferably with dark orange flesh, or
   butternut squash, cut into chunks
A few tablespoons of extra virgin olive oil if roasting the pumpkin
Salt and freshly ground black pepper
1 egg, lightly beaten
250g (9 oz) ricotta cheese
100g (4 oz) Parmesan or asiago cheese, freshly grated
Nutmeg for grating
1–2 amaretti biscuits, crumbled

Either steam the pumpkin to cook it, or preheat the oven to 190°C/375°F/Gas 5 and roast it: place the chunks on a baking sheet, drizzle with some olive oil, salt and pepper, cover with foil and roast for about 30 minutes or until cooked through. Leave until cool enough to handle, scrape the pumpkin away from the peel and purée the flesh.

Combine the pumpkin purée with the egg, ricotta cheese, Parmesan or asiago and grated nutmeg and season to taste. The consistency should be soft but not so runny that it will ooze out of its pasta case. Stir in the amaretti and chill for at least 30

minutes.

To fill the ravioli, hold a pasta square or round in one hand, brush water around the edge and place a tablespoon of the filling in the centre, then top with a second piece of pasta. Pinch the edges to seal. Leave on a floured plate or board for at least 10 minutes to allow the seal to set. Repeat until all the ravioli have been filled.

In a sauté pan, gently heat the butter with the sage until it melts and sizzles and is infused with the flavour of the leaves. Remove from the heat before it browns or burns, and set aside.

Bring a large pan of salted water to the boil and gently simmer the ravioli for 2–3 minutes. Using a slotted spoon, lift them out of the cooking water individually, then carefully pat dry with kitchen paper or an absorbent clean tea-cloth.

Drizzle a little of the sage butter on to a warm serving platter along with some extra grated Parmesan, then top with the hot ravioli, more butter and sage leaves, Parmesan and the pine nuts. Serve right away.

VARIATION

Cannelloni di Zucca con Tartufi
Truffled Pumpkin Cannelloni

Instead of making ravioli, add a drizzle of truffle oil to the pumpkin filling and stuff it into cannelloni tubes. Use either dried cannelloni which you parboil then drain, rinse in cold water and fill, or lasagne sheets which you parboil, drain, rinse in cool water for easy handling then roll around the filling. You can also use wonton wrappers which don't need parboiling: simply roll them around the filling and pour a few tablespoons of water over the top before baking.

Preheat the oven to 190°C/375°F/Gas 5 and place the pumpkin-filled cannelloni in a baking dish, to fit snugly, with a little water or stock poured over the top. Omitting the sage leaves, dot the top with butter, grate over some Parmesan and cover tightly with foil. Bake for about 15 minutes then remove the foil and bake for a further 10 minutes or long enough to lightly toast the top.

Gnocchi di Spinaci con Salsa al Gorgonzola

Spinach Gnocchi with Gorgonzola Sauce

We ate this dish of tasty gnocchi in San Gimignano, the ancient walled city in Tuscany. The little cobbled streets are lined with food shops, each one offering a wide variety of local specialities.

SERVES 4

500g (1lb 2 oz) fresh spinach, or 250g (9 oz) frozen spinach, defrosted
250g (9 oz) potatoes, peeled and cut into chunks
Salt and freshly ground black pepper
1 egg, lightly beaten
100g (4 oz) Parmesan or pecorino cheese, freshly grated
6–8 tablespoons plain flour, or as needed
Pinch of freshly grated nutmeg
100g (4 oz) Gorgonzola or Roquefort cheese, crumbled
3–4 tablespoons double or single cream
Few drops of lemon juice

Cook the spinach in a large pan with a tiny amount of water for only a few moments or until it is bright green. Drain well, leave to cool, then chop and set aside. Cook the potato chunks in rapidly boiling salted water until tender. Drain and mash coarsely.

Combine the spinach and potatoes with the egg and cheese, then work in the flour, nutmeg, and salt and pepper. Work it until it forms a stiff dough.

With floured hands, pull off small plum-sized or large walnut-sized chunks of dough and roll each one into a ball then into a rope 2.5cm (1 in) in diameter. Working on a floured board, using a paring knife, cut the rope of dough into 2–2.5cm (¾–1 in) lengths. Toss these in more flour and arrange on a floured board or plate. When the surface is covered with one layer of gnocchi, cover with plastic wrap and place the next layer on top, until all the dough is rolled and cut.

Bring a large pan of salted water to the boil and add the gnocchi a few at a time, reducing the heat to a simmer. Cover and gently simmer for about 5 minutes – the gnocchi will fall to the bottom and then rise to the top when they're cooked. Spoon them out and leave them to drain on a plate or baking sheet.

Warm the Gorgonzola or Roquefort very gently in a small pan with the cream until blended and toss with the drained gnocchi. Squeeze a few drops of lemon juice over the top and serve immediately.

Stelle di Formaggio di Capra

Chilli Goat's Cheese Pasta 'Stars' in Tomato and Ginger Salsa

Asian pasta wrappers, such as gyoza or wonton, are perfect for quick, home-made, filled dumplings. Here the edges of the wrappers are pinched around spicy and herby goat's cheese, to form star shapes. Steamed and served on a wonderful sauce of tomato and ginger, they are as delightful to look at as to taste.

Both the sauce and dumplings can be prepared in advance and reheated (either in a steamer or microwave) before serving.

SERVES 4 as a starter. Double the recipe for larger (or should I say greedier?) appetites.

175g (6 oz), approximately, mild goat's cheese such as Montrachet, crumbled
3 tablespoons freshly chopped coriander
½ fresh green chilli such as jalapeño, or to taste
2 cloves garlic, chopped
4 tablespoons coarsely grated or shredded Pecorino, asiago, or Parmesan cheese
12 gyoza or wonton wrappers, or 6–8cm (2½–3 in) diameter pasta rounds
1 tablespoon olive oil

For the salsa
40g (1½ oz) butter
8 very ripe, flavourful fresh tomatoes, chopped (not canned)
About 1 tablespoon chopped fresh root ginger, or to taste
Salt to taste
Pinch of sugar, if needed
2 cloves garlic, chopped
1–2 spring onions, thinly sliced

Combine the goat's cheese with the coriander, green chilli, garlic and the cheese and mix well.

Take a gyoza wrapper in one hand and brush water around the edge. Place a tablespoon or so of cheese mixture in the centre of the wrapper and pinch the edges tightly together into the centre to form a star or flower-like shape. Repeat until all of the dumplings have been filled and then dip the bottom of each one in the olive oil to prevent them sticking to the steamer.

Bring a steamer of water to the boil. Arrange the dumplings in the top and cover

tightly. Leave them to steam over a high heat until they are cooked through, about 3–5 minutes.

Meanwhile, for the salsa, heat the butter in a pan with the tomatoes and ginger. Season with salt, and sugar if needed. When the butter has melted and the tomatoes have cooked slightly, remove them from the heat and stir in the garlic and spring onion.

Spoon the warm tomato and ginger salsa on to serving plates, then carefully lift the dumplings out of the steamer and arrange them on top. Serve immediately.

VARIATION

Ravioli con Agnello e Spezie di Marocco
Cumin and Coriander Ravioli in Tomato and Ginger Salsa

Totally delicious, this pasta is filled with a North African-inspired lamb filling.

Instead of the cheese filling, mix about 600g (1 lb 5 oz) minced lamb with 8 finely chopped cloves garlic, 2 beaten eggs, a teaspoon or two of ground cumin, a splash of hot sauce, such as Tabasco, or cayenne pepper, and several tablespoons of chopped coriander leaves. Add salt to taste and some fresh breadcrumbs, if the mixture needs binding, and seal as for ravioli. Cook gently in lightly boiling water for about 4 minutes, until the meat is no longer pink inside and is still deliciously juicy. Serve with the salsa as above.

Gnocchi alle Verdure Estive

Gnocchi with Summer Vegetables

We spent an afternoon in Rome wandering through the sun-baked streets, past a man singing opera, stopping in cafés where the chic and trendy sit under sun umbrellas, then on, past cooling fountains and friendly dogs. We walked until we could walk no more, then we ducked into the nearest little trattoria *and ate a big dish of this gnocchi with lots of vegetables in a buttery tomato sauce.*

SERVES 4

2 small courgettes, preferably a combination of both green and yellow, thinly sliced or cut into juliennes
1 tablespoon extra virgin olive oil
3 cloves garlic, chopped
3–5 blanched artichoke hearts, quartered or sliced, or about 10 spears of asparagus, cut into bite-sized pieces and blanched
Handful of sugar-snap peas, or fresh, young, blanched shelled peas
3 heaped tablespoons tomato purée
450g (1 lb) potato gnocchi
1 teaspoon each of freshly chopped marjoram and rosemary
30–40g (1–1½ oz) unsalted butter
Salt and freshly ground black pepper
3–4 tablespoons freshly grated Parmesan or pecorino cheese

Gently sauté the courgettes in the olive oil in a large pan for about 5 minutes until they are lightly browned and soft, then add the garlic, artichoke hearts or asparagus and sugar-snap peas or shelled peas. Cook for 2–3 minutes and stir in the tomato purée. Cover and remove from the heat.

Cook the gnocchi for about 3 minutes in a large pan of rapidly boiling salted water until just tender, then drain carefully so that they don't fall apart.

Toss the gnocchi with the vegetables, herbs, butter and salt and pepper to taste, then sprinkle with the cheese. Heap on to a platter or into soup bowls and serve right away.

Ravioli alla Dr Leah con Formaggio di Capra e Tartufi

Dr Leah's Truffled Goat's Cheese Ravioli

The luxurious ravioli filling of truffled goat's cheese was inspired by a visit to Alba, in Italy's Piedmont, one October – the truffle season. This delicacy was part of a celebration feast when my daughter Leah became a doctor.
SERVES 4–6

300g (11 oz) fresh white goat's cheese, crumbled
3 cloves garlic, finely chopped
1–2 tablespoons truffle oil, or to taste
1–2 fresh or canned truffles, finely chopped, including juice (optional)
2 egg yolks, lightly beaten
350g (12 oz) wonton wrappers or fresh pasta sheets, cut into 10–15cm
    (4–6 in) squares (enough for 3–4 big, fat ravioli per person)
Salt and freshly ground black pepper
350ml (12 fl oz) double cream
Nutmeg for grating
4–6 tablespoons freshly grated Parmesan cheese
30–40g (1–1½ oz) unsalted butter

In a bowl, mash together the goat's cheese, garlic, half the truffle oil, half the truffles, if using, and the egg yolks. Take a piece of pasta and place a tablespoon or two of the goat's cheese filling in the centre. Brush the edges with water. Lightly brush the edges of a second piece of pasta with water and place it, moist edges down, over the filling, sealing it to make a parcel, while at the same time pressing out any excess air. Cover a large baking sheet with plastic wrap and dust it with flour. Place each ravioli on the sheet as you make them.

Bring a very large pan of salted water to the boil. Meanwhile, prepare a large ovenproof dish for serving: warm it in a very low oven first. Season the cream with grated nutmeg, salt and pepper and drizzle a little of it across the bottom of the dish, sprinkle some of the Parmesan over and return it to the oven to keep warm.

When the water has reached a rapid boil, carefully drop the ravioli into the water a few at a time and leave them to cook for about 3 minutes until they are just tender. Once cooked, lift each one out with a slotted spoon, allowing the excess water to drip away for a moment or two, then transfer to the warm serving dish. Drizzle the remaining cream and cheese over the top, along with the remaining truffle oil and truffles. Serve dotted with tiny pieces of butter, and fork your way to heaven.

Tortellini al Forno con Panna e Piselli

Baked Tortellini in Cream with Peas

An utterly comforting, soothingly rich and creamy dish, perfumed with nutmeg and sweetened with peas – it takes mere minutes to prepare.

For this dish to be so good that it makes you want to rip off your clothes and roll around naked, use really good quality tortellini imported from Italy. Sad to say that most of the supermarket stuffed pastas I've tasted are doughy, heavy and have fillings that are, at their best, bland and uninteresting.

SERVES 4

About 400g (14 oz) fresh tortellini or 300–350g (11–12 oz) dried
100ml (4 fl oz) vegetable stock
350ml (12 fl oz) whipping cream
Salt and freshly ground black pepper
Nutmeg for grating
Handful of tiny fresh, blanched, shelled peas or frozen petits pois
4–6 tablespoons freshly grated Parmesan cheese, plus extra for serving
15–30g (½–1 oz) butter

Preheat the oven to 200°C/400°F/Gas 6.

Cook the pasta in a large pan of rapidly boiling salted water until just *al dente*, then drain lightly.

Pour a few tablespoons of the vegetable stock and about a third of the cream into a shallow ovenproof baking or gratin dish – roughly 30 x 20 x 4cm (12 x 8 x 1½ in) – then sprinkle with salt, pepper and some grated nutmeg and scatter half of the peas and Parmesan over the top. Tip in the tortellini, then pour over the remaining stock and cream and add more salt and pepper, nutmeg and the rest of the peas. Top with the remaining Parmesan.

Give the dish a little shake or a slight stir, to distribute the ingredients. Dot the top with butter, cover and bake for 5 minutes, then remove the cover and bake for a further 5–10 minutes or until the top is lightly golden and the cream bubbling and thick.

Serve right away with some extra Parmesan for grating as desired.

Ravioli Verdi con Zucchine Gialle, Fagioli Rosa e Salsa al Peperoncino

Green Ravioli with Yellow Squash, Pink Beans and Chilli Sauce

This is one of the few fusion pasta recipes I've allowed myself in this collection of molto Italiano *recipes – it's delicious, easy to make and healthy as well. And who says the Italians only like traditional Italian flavours? I've noticed that the spicy flavours of cumin, curry, fresh coriander and lime are increasingly making their way on to the Italian table.*
SERVES 4

350–450g (12 oz–1 lb) young yellow courgettes, sliced into 3–6mm (⅛–¼ in) pieces
2–3 tablespoons olive oil
3–4 cloves garlic, finely chopped
400g (14 oz) cooked and drained, or canned, borlotti beans
350ml (12 fl oz) vegetable or chicken stock
1 tablespoon or more mild red chilli powder (I use a peperoncino with a rich though quite spicy flavour, mixed with 2 teaspoons paprika)
½ teaspoon cumin, or to taste
Juice of ½ lime
Salt and freshly ground black pepper
350–450g (12 oz–1 lb) green ravioli filled with spinach and ricotta cheese
3–4 spring onions, thinly sliced
2–3 tablespoons coarsely chopped coriander leaves
Freshly grated Parmesan or pecorino cheese, as desired

Lightly sauté the courgettes in the olive oil in a large pan until lightly gilded, then sprinkle with the garlic and cook for a moment longer.

Add the beans and stir together with the courgettes, then pour in the stock and add the spices and lime juice. Season to taste and keep warm while you cook the pasta.

In a large pan of rapidly boiling water, cook the ravioli until *al dente*. Drain, reserving a few tablespoons of the cooking liquid, and toss gently with the courgette and bean mixture, adding the cooking liquid if it needs more moisture.

Serve with the spring onions, coriander and grated cheese sprinkled lavishly over the top.

Index

Note: Page numbers in **bold** refer to major text sections, those in *italic* to illustrations. Vegetarian recipes are shown in **bold** text. The English title only of each recipe is listed in subheadings.

Acquacotta alla Scansano 28, 29
Acquacotta con Pasta e Rucola 26, *27*
anchovies *see* fish
Anelli al Forno 155
Angel Hair Pasta, Prawns and Roasted-tomato Sauce 54
asparagus
   Asparagus Soup with Ravioli 34
   Asparagus Soup with Star-shaped Pasta 31
aubergines
   Aubergine Turbans Filled with Ditalini 166–7, *167*
   Bucatini with Aubergine and Roasted-tomato Sauce 54
   Sicilian Pasta with Aubergine 74

bacon *see* meats and poultry
baked pasta **154–72**
   Aubergine Turbans Filled with Ditalini 166–7, *167*
   Baked Macaroni with Cauliflower and Ricotta 172
   Baked Pasta and Cheeses with Beetroot Pesto 170, *171*
   Baked Ravioli with Rosemary-tomato Sauce *158*, 159
   Cannelloni Filled with Spinach and Ricotta, Baked with Tomatoes and Basil 156–7
   Cannelloni Filled with Turkey,

Chicken Liver and Ham 160–61
   Cannelloni with Meat and Spinach Filling 157
   Lasagne with Béchamel, Cheese, Vegetables and Prosciutto 168–9
   Lasagne with Peas, Tomato Sauce and Béchamel 164–5
   Pasta Rings Baked with Peas, Meat and Cheese 155
   Shell Pasta with Roasted Chicken 162–3, *163*
   Baked Ravioli with Rosemary-tomato Sauce *158*, 159
   Baked Tortellini in Cream with Peas 186
basil 20
Bavette o Orecchiette con Gamberetti e Zucchine 108
beans 20
   Broad Bean and Potato Soup with Tomatoes and Ditalini 30
   Pasta and Bean Soup 42, *43*
   Yellow and Green Bean Soup with Ditalini 32, *33*
beef *see* meats and poultry
breadcrumbs 20
   Broad Bean and Potato Soup with Tomatoes and Ditalini 30
broccoli, Spaghetti and Broccoli Soup 25
Bucatini con Melanzane e Pomodori Arrosto 54
Bucatini with Aubergine and Roasted-tomato Sauce 54
Butterfly Pasta with Walnut Sauce *64*, 65

Cannelloni all' Aeoliana 156–7
Cannelloni alla Pesaro 160–61
Cannelloni di Ricotta in Salsa di Peperoni con Tartufo 174–5, *175*
Cannelloni di Zucca con

Tartufi 178
Cannelloni Filled with Spinach and Ricotta, Baked with Tomatoes and Basil 156–7
Cannelloni Filled with Turkey, Chicken Liver and Ham 160–61
Cannelloni Terrestri 157
Cannelloni with Meat and Spinach Filling 157
Capelli d'Angelo con Gamberi e Pomodori Arrosto 54
capers 20
Caserecci con Pesto Trapanese 63
cheese *see* dairy products, etc
chicken *see* meats and poultry
Chickpea Soup with Fettuccine 44
Chickpea Soup with Orzo 25
Chilli Goat's Cheese Pasta 'Stars' in Tomato and Ginger Salsa 180–82, *181*
chillies 21
clams *see* seafood
Classic Spaghetti with Garlic and Anchovies 146
Cold Pasta for Shabbat 152
Cold Pasta with Aubergine 152
Conchiglie ai Formaggi 144
Conchiglie con Pollo Arrosto 162–3, *163*
Cool Pasta with Courgettes and Baby Octopus 70
Cool Pasta with Courgettes and Rocket 70
Courgette Soup with Pasta, White Wine and Fresh Herbs 40
crawfish *see* seafood
Crema di Asparagi con Ravioli 34
Cumin and Coriander Ravioli in Tomato and Ginger Salsa 182

dairy products **78–92**
   cheese 20–21

Farfalle with Ricotta and Spring Onions 79
Little Pasta Ears with Spicy Tomato Sauce, Peas and Cheese 87
Nigel's Green Pasta with Goat's Cheddar and Fresh Basil Oil 80, *81*
Pappardelle with Pan-roasted Vegetables and Ricotta 90–91
Pappardelle with Rosemary Butter 92
Pasta with Ricotta, Goat's Cheese and Rocket *84*, 85
Pasta with Sun-dried Tomato and Goat's Cheese Pesto 86
Tagliarini with Rosemary Cream in a Crisp Parmesan Bowl 82-3
Tagliatelle in Saffron Cream with Prosciutto 88, *89*
Dr Leah's Truffled Goat's Cheese Ravioli 184, *185*
dried pasta *see* pasta

Farfalle con Pesto d'Invernale *64*, 65
Farfalle con Ricotta 79
Farfalle with Ricotta and Spring Onions 79
Fat Spaghetti with Bay-scented Lemon Sauce 52
Fat Spaghetti with Spicy Cauliflower and Sausage Sauce 129
Fat Pasta Twists with Sicilian-style Pesto Sauce 63
Fettuccine al Gorgonzola, Pesto e Mascarpone 136
Fettuccine alla Papalina 122, 123
Fettuccine Boscaiole 48-9
Fettuccine con Aragosta e Fave 105
Fettuccine con Granchi e Piselli 101
Fettuccine with Mushrooms and Truffle Oil 48–9
Fettuccine Voluttuose 124–5
Fettuccine with a Voluptuous Sauce of Duck and Porcini 124–5
Fettuccine with Creamy Crab and Peas 101
Fettuccine with Gorgonzola,

Pesto and Mascarpone 136
Fettuccine with Lobster and Broad Beans 105
Fettuccine with Peas, Prosciutto and Raw Egg *122*, 123
fish *see* seafood
Fresh Egg Pasta 15-6
Fresh Eggless Pasta 14
Fresh Tomato Sauce from Napoli 18

garlic 21–2
Garlic and Sage Soup with Pastina 35
Garlicky Tagliatelle with Fresh Herbs 60, *61*
Gemelli alla Caprese 50, *51*
Gemelli con Pomodori Arrosto, Gorgonzola e Basilico 55
Gemelli with Roasted-tomato Sauce, Blue Cheese and Basil 55
gnocchi *see* stuffed pasta and gnocchi
Gnocchi alle Verdure Estive 183
Gnocchi di Spinaci con Salsa al Gorgonzola 179
Goat's Cheese Raviolini in Chicken Soup 25
Green Pesto Minestrone *38*, 39
Green Ravioli with Yellow Squash, Pink Beans and Chilli Sauce 187

ham *see* meats and poultry
herbs 20, 22

Insalata di Orzo, Zucchine e Rucola 70
Insalata di Pasta e Zucchine con Polpo 70

lamb *see* meats and poultry
langoustines *see* seafood
Lasagne alla Veneziana 164–5
Lasagne Bianche alla Spoleto 168–9
Lasagne with Béchamel,

Cheese, Vegetables and Prosciutto 168–9
Lasagne with Peas, Tomato Sauce and Béchamel 164–5
Linguine con Tonno e Limone 112
Linguine with Tuna and Lemon 112
Little Ears with Broccoli Sauce 59
Little Pasta Ears with Spicy Tomato Sauce, Peas and Cheese 87

Maccheroni alla Libanese 141
Maccheroni con Salsa Messicana 76, *77*
machines, pasta 16
Marlena's Mexican Fusion Pasta Bowl *76*, *77*
meats and poultry **117–34**
Baked Ravioli with Rosemary-tomato Sauce *158*, 159
Cannelloni Filled with Turkey, Chicken Liver and Ham 160–61
Cannelloni with Meat and Spinach Filling 157
Cumin and Coriander Ravioli in Tomato and Ginger Salsa 182
Fat Spaghetti with Spicy Cauliflower and Sausage Sauce 129
Fettuccine with a Voluptuous Sauce of Duck and Porcini 124–5
Fettuccine with Peas, Prosciutto and Raw Egg *122*, 123
Lasagne with Béchamel, Cheese, Vegetables and Prosciutto 168–9
Pasta Abruzzo-style with Prosciutto and Courgettes 132–3
Pasta Rings Baked with Tomatoes, Peas, Meat and Cheese 155
Pasta with Braised Chicken Thighs, Spicy Tomato Sauce, Meat and Spinach 126–7, *127*
Pasta with Meaty Tomato and Fennel Sauce 128
Ribbons of Pasta with an Old-fashioned Ragù Sauce 121

Rigatoni with a Sauce of Rabbit, Spinach and Porcini 120

Shell Pasta with Roasted Chicken 162–3, *163*

Spaghetti alla Carbonara 134

Spaghetti with Sausage, Olives and Marsala 130, *131*

Spaghetti with Spicy Lamb Sauce 118, *119*

Spaghetti with Spinach, Lemon and Pancetta 62

Tagliatelle in Saffron Cream with Prosciutto 88, *89*

Midnight Pasta 140

Minestra con Aglio e Salvia 35

Minestra di Asparagi con Stelline 31

Minestra di Ceci e Orzo 25

Minestra di Fave e Ditalini 30

Minestra di Pasta e Broccoli 25

Minestra di Zucchine 40

Minestra Giardiniera 32, *33*

Minestrone Verde alla Genovese *38*, *39*

mushrooms, **Pasta with Porcini** 66

Nigel's Green Pasta with Goat's Cheddar and Fresh Basil Oil 80, *81*

nutmeg 22

octopus *see* seafood

olives 22

oil/paste 19, 22

Orecchiette alla Contadina 87

Orecchiette con Broccoli 59

oregano 22

pancetta *see* meats and poultry

Pappardelle al Sugo Antico 121

Pappardelle con Burro al Rosmarino 92

Pappardelle con Verdure Grigliate e Ricotta 90–91

Pappardelle with Pan-roasted Vegetables and Ricotta 90–91

Pappardelle with Rosemary Butter 92

pasta **9–16**

cooking 13

dried 10–11, 13

fresh 10–11, 13, 14–16

making **13–16**

Egg Pasta 15–16

Eggless Pasta 14

pasta machines 16

shapes and sizes 11–12

Pasta Abruzzo-style with Prosciutto and Courgettes 132–3

Pasta ai Funghi 66

Pasta al Basilico 15

Pasta al Forno con Formaggio 170, *171*

Pasta al Pomodoro e Pesto 137

Pasta alla 'Nigel' 80, *81*

Pasta alla Norma 74

Pasta alla Siracusana 75

Pasta all'Erbe 15

Pasta alle Zucchine con Salsa di Peperoni 138, *139*

Pasta allo Zafferano 15

Pasta allo Zafferano e Rucola 148

Pasta all'Uovo Fresca 15–16

Pasta and Bean Soup 42, *43*

Pasta and Roasted-tomato Sauce 53–5

pasta asciutto see pasta, dried

Pasta Caprina 86

Pasta con Cappe Sante 104

Pasta con Cavolfiore e Ricotta 172

Pasta con Gamberi 98, 99–100

Pasta con le Sarde 114–16, *115*

Pasta con Pomodoro Arrostiti 53–5

Pasta con Ragù alla Paesana 126–7, *127*

Pasta dei Pastori 84, 85

Pasta di Ferragosto 46, 47

Pasta di Mezzanotte 140

Pasta e Ceci 44

Pasta e Fagioli 42, *43*

Pasta for a Hot Summer's Day 46, 47

Pasta Fredda alla Giudea 152

Pasta Fredda con Melanzane 152

Pasta Fresca 14

pasta fresca see pasta, fresh

Pasta Mezzogiorno 128

Pasta Mista e Lenticchie 41

Pasta Neri 104

Pasta Piccante Abruzzese con Prosciutto e Zucchine 132–3

Pasta Quills with Peas and Mushrooms in Creamy Tomato Sauce 67

Pasta Rings Baked with Peas, Meat and Cheese 155

Pasta Rossa 16

pasta sciue-sciue see quick, quick pasta

Pasta Shells with Emmenthal and Crème Fraîche 144

Pasta Tubes Filled with Ricotta, in a Spicy Red-pepper Sauce with Truffle 174–5, *175*

Pasta Tubes with Mixed Peppers and Courgettes 72, *73*

Pasta Twists with Cherry Tomatoes, Mozzarella and Basil 50, *51*

Pasta Verde 16

Pasta Wheels with Aubergine, Peppers, Capers, Olives and Tomatoes 75

Pasta with Braised Chicken Thighs, Spicy Tomato Sauce, Meat and Spinach 126–7, *127*

Pasta with Courgettes and Red-pepper Sauce 138, *139*

Pasta with Lentils 41

Pasta with Mascarpone and Smoked Salmon 110, *111*

Pasta with Meaty Tomato and Fennel Sauce 128

Pasta with Porcini 66

Pasta with Prawns and Courgettes 108

Pasta with Ricotta, Goat's Cheese and Rocket 84, 85

Pasta with Sardines 114–16, *115*

Pasta with Spicy Sardinian Prawn Sauce *98*, 99–100

Pasta with Sun-dried Tomato and Goat's Cheese Pesto 86

Pasta with Tomato Sauce and Pesto 137

Pasticcio di Ravioli al Rosmarino 158, *159*

Penne al Limone e Peperoncino 56, *57*

Penne con Fagiolini, Olive e Pomodori Arrosto 54

Penne con Peperoni, Finocchi e Pomodori Arrosto 55

Penne con Zucchine 149

Penne Rigate con Piselli e Funghi in Salsa Rossa 67

Penne with Courgettes, Carbonara-style 149

Penne with Green Beans, Olives and Roasted-tomato Sauce 54
Penne with Lemon and Chilli 56, 57
Penne with Roasted Peppers, Fennel and Roasted-tomato Sauce 55
pepper 19
Perciatelli con Cavolfiore e Salsicce 129
Pesce all' Isolana 109
pesto sauces 18–19, 22–3
Pesto 19
pork *see* meats and poultry
poultry *see* meats and poultry
prawns *see* seafood
prosciutto *see* meats and poultry
Pumpkin Ravioli with Butter, Sage and Parmesan 176–8, *177*

quick, quick pasta **135–53**
Classic Spaghetti with Garlic and Anchovies 146
Cold Pasta for Shabbat 152
Cold Pasta with Aubergine 152
Fettuccine with Gorgonzola, Pesto and Mascarpone 136
Midnight Pasta 140
Pasta Shells with Emmenthal and Crème Fraîche 144
Pasta with Courgettes and Red-pepper Sauce 138, *139*
Pasta with Tomato Sauce and Pesto 137
Penne with Courgettes, Carbonara-style 149
Small Pasta with Basil, Parsley and Lime 141
Spaghetti or Trofie with Walnuts and Parmesan 142, *143*
Spaghetti with Anchovies and Breadcrumbs 153
Spaghetti with Cheese and Black Pepper 145
Spaghetti with Garlic, Oil and Hot Pepper 146, *147*
Thin Spaghetti with Sun-dried Tomatoes 150, *151*
Tuscan Pasta with Saffron and Rocket 148

rabbit *see* meats and poultry
Ravioli alla Dr Leah con Formaggio di Capra e Tartufi 184, *185*
Ravioli con Angello e Spezie del Marocco 182
Ravioli di Zucca alla Mantovana con Salvia 176–8, *177*
Ravioli Verdi con Zucchine Gialle, Fagioli Rosa e Salsa al Peperoncino 187
Raviolini con Formaggio di Capra in Brodo di Pollo 25
Real Pasta with Pesto, The 58
Red Snapper with Peas and Saffron Pastina 'Pearls' 109
Ribbons of Pasta with an Old-fashioned Ragù Sauce 121
Rigatoni con Salsa di Coniglio, Spinaci e Porcini 120
Rigatoni with a Sauce of Rabbit, Spinach and Porcini 120
Shell Pasta with Roasted Chicken 162–3, *163*

saffron 23
Pasta allo Zafferano 15
salmon *see* seafood
Salsa al Pomodoro e Basilico 17
Salsa di Pomodori Freschi 18
Salsa di Pomodoro 17
salt 19
sardines *see* seafood
sauces *see* pesto sauces; tomato sauce
scallops *see* seafood
shellfish *see* seafood
Shell Pasta with Roasted Chicken 162–3, *63*
seafood 20, 23, **93–116**
Angel Hair Pasta, Prawns and Roasted-tomato Sauce 54
Classic Spaghetti with Garlic and Anchovies 146
Cool Pasta with Courgettes and Baby Octopus 70
Fettuccine with Creamy Crab and Peas 101
Fettuccine with Lobster and Broad Beans 105
Linguine with Tuna and Lemon 112
Pasta with Mascarpone and Smoked Salmon 110, *111*

Pasta with Prawns and Courgettes 108
Pasta with Sardines 114–16, *115*
Pasta with Spicy Sardinian Prawn Sauce 98, *99*–100
Red Snapper with Peas and Saffron Pastina 'Pearls' 109
Scallops with Black Squid-ink Pasta 104
Soup of Clams and Tiny Pasta 36, *37*
Spaghetti with Anchovies and Breadcrumbs 153
Spaghetti with Clams, Neopolitan-style 94, *95*
Spaghetti with Langoustines, Crawfish or Prawns *102*, 103–4
Spaghetti with Mixed Seafood and Spicy Tomato Sauce 96–7
Spaghetti with Squid and Peas 113
Ziti with Swordfish and Mint 106, *107*
Sicilian Pasta with Aubergine 74
Small Pasta with Basil, Parsley and Lime 141
snapper *see* fish
soup **24–44**
Asparagus Soup with Ravioli 34
Asparagus Soup with Star-shaped Pasta 31
Broad Bean and Potato Soup with Tomatoes and Ditalini 30
Chickpea Soup with Fettuccine 44
Chickpea Soup with Orzo 25
Courgette Soup with Pasta, White Wine and Fresh Herbs 40
Garlic and Sage Soup with Pastina 35
Goat's Cheese Raviolini in Chicken Soup 25
Green Pesto Minestrone *38*, 39
Pasta and Bean Soup 42, *43*
Pasta with Lentils 41
Soup of Clams and Tiny Pasta 36, *37*
Spaghetti and Broccoli Soup 25
Tuscan Spinach Soup with

Porcini, White Beans and Shells *28*, *29*
Tuscan Tomato and Potato Soup with Pasta and Rocket 26, *27*
Yellow and Green Bean Soup with Ditalini 32, *33*
Spaghetti agli Spinaci 62
Spaghetti Aglio, Olio e Alici 146
Spaghetti Aglio, Olio e Peperoncino 146, *147*
Spaghetti ai Frutti di Mare 96–7
Spaghetti ai Peperoncini Verdi 71
Spaghetti al Marsala 130, *131*
Spaghetti alla Carbonara 134
Spaghetti alle Vongole 94, *95*
Spaghetti con Alici 153
Spaghetti con Aragosta o Gamberi 102, 103–4
Spaghetti con Cacio e Pepe 145
Spaghetti con Calamari e Piselli 113
Spaghetti con Pomodori Arrosto e Broccoli alla Campagnola 55
Spaghetti con Sugo D'Agnello 118, *119*
Spaghetti o Trofie con Noci e Parmigiano 142, *143*
Spaghetti or Trofie with Walnuts and Parmesan 142, *143*
Spaghetti Tartufati con Asparagi e Uova 68, *69*
Spaghetti with Anchovies and Breadcrumbs 153
Spaghetti and Broccoli Soup 25
Spaghetti with Cheese and Black Pepper 145
Spaghetti with Clams, Neapolitan-style 94, *95*
Spaghetti with Garlic, Oil and Hot Pepper 146, *147*
Spaghetti with Green Italian Peppers 71
Spaghetti with Langoustines, Crawfish or Prawns *102*, 103–4
Spaghetti with Mixed Seafood and Spicy Tomato Sauce 96–7
Spaghetti with Roasted-tomato Sauce and Broccoli 55
Spaghetti with Sausage, Olives and Marsala 130, *131*

Spaghetti with Spicy Lamb Sauce 118, *119*
Spaghetti with Spinach, Lemon and Pancetta 62
Spaghetti with Squid and Peas 113
Spaghettini ai Pomodori Secchi 150, *151*
spinach
Spinach Gnocchi with Gorgonzola Sauce 179
Tuscan Spinach Soup with Porcini, White Beans and Shells *28*, *29*
squid *see* seafood
Stelle di Formaggio di Capra 180–82, *181*
stock 23
Strangozzi al Limone 52
stuffed pasta and gnocchi **173–89**
Baked Tortellini in Cream with Peas 186
Chilli Goat's Cheese Pasta 'Stars' in Tomato and Ginger Salsa 180–82, *181*
Cumin and Coriander Ravioli in Ginger and Tomato Salsa 182
Dr Leah's Truffled Goat's Cheese Ravioli 184, *185*
Gnocchi with Summer Vegetables 183
Green Ravioli with Yellow Squash, Pink Beans and Chilli Sauce 187
Pasta Tubes Filled with Ricotta, in a Spicy Red-pepper Sauce with Truffle 174–5, *175*
Pumpkin Ravioli with Butter, Sage and Parmesan 176–8, *177*
Spinach Gnocchi with Gorgonzola Sauce 179
Truffled Pumpkin Cannelloni 178
sun-dried vegetables 23
swordfish *see* seafood

Tagliarini al Rosmarino in Nidi di Parmigiano 82-3
Tagliarini with Rosemary Cream in a Crisp Parmesan Bowl 82-3
Tagliatelle alle Erbe 60, *61*
Tagliatelle allo Zafferano 88, *89*

Tagliatelle in Saffron Cream with Prosciutto 88, *89*
Tagliolini al Salmone Affumicato 110, *111*
Thin Spaghetti with Sun-dried Tomatoes 150, *151*
Timballi di Melanzane con Ditalini 166–7, *167*
tomato sauce 16–18
Fresh Tomato Sauce from Napoli 18
Tomato Sauce 17
Tomato Sauce with Basil 17
tomatoes 23
Tortellini al Forno con Panna e Piselli al Forno 186
Tortiglioni con Peperoni e Zucchine 72, *73*
Trofie o Trenette al Pesto 58
Truffled Pumpkin Cannelloni 178
Truffled Spaghetti with Asparagus and Egg 68, *69*
tuna *see* seafood
turkey *see* meats and poultry
Tuscan Pasta with Saffron and Rocket 148
Tuscan Pesto 19
Tuscan Spinach Soup with Porcini, White Beans and Shells *28*, *29*
Tuscan Tomato and Potato Soup with Pasta and Rocket 26, *27*

vegetable dishes **45–77**
note: vegetables form a major part of many recipes throughout the book
vegetables, sun-dried 23
vegetarian dishes are indicated by **bold** text throughout the index

Yellow and Green Bean Soup with Ditalini 32, *33*

Ziti con Pesce Spada e Menta 106, *107*
Ziti with Swordfish and Mint 106, *107*
Zuppa di Vongole e Fregula 36, *37*